STUFFING

Personalize poultry, meat, fish, and vegetable main dishes with flavorful combinations.

There are so many different types of stuffing mixtures that can be prepared, especially for filling the traditional roast turkey, that it is difficult to advise someone which one to choose. It seems that the type of stuffing you prefer is often as personal as your own name. To some, the typical stuffing, or dressing as it is often called, is a moist, highly seasoned bread mixture tucked inside of a turkey, while to others, it is a drier, mildly flavored corn bread combination.

When the word stuffing is mentioned, many homemakers immediately associate it with turkey. The use of stuffing is not really so limited. In fact, stuffings are used to add or heighten the flavor of vegetables, fish, and many other meats. Stuffings are so popular that sometimes stuffing mixtures are even cooked and served without being put into other food.

Stuffing one food with another is not a new cooking technique, for according to Herodotus, a fifth century B.C. Greek historian, the people of Egypt stuffed a sacrificial bull with items including bread, honey, figs, and raisins. After the animal had been offered to the gods, the meat was eaten by the celebrants. Undoubtedly, the people of other countries also stuffed animals prior to roasting them.

Some of the early stuffed animals were served quite elegantly. In England, spice-stuffed peacock was served at royal feasts. Before roasting, the skin was removed, then after roasting it was sewn back on. The multicolored tail feathers were spread out on the platter.

Some of the earlier cook books and some present-day foreign cook books refer to stuffings as forcemeats. This word comes from the French word *farcier* which means to stuff. However, forcemeats are not always used as stuffings and oftentimes stand alone as chopped mixtures.

Stuffings play an important role in cooking even today. They not only add variety to menus, but they have four major functions in cooking. Stuffings add flavor, prevent many of the flavorful juices from escaping, help retain the shape of the food that is being stuffed, and they also are a means of stretching the amount of food that is being served.

The flavor that stuffings impart can be distinctive, depending on the mixture. For example, such herbs as sage affect the overall flavor of the dish. Fruits also are complementary flavors frequently added to poultry stuffings. Apples and onions are often used to stuff oily birds, such as ducks or geese, to absorb the grease. The stuffing is generally discarded after roasting.

Stuffings also soak up the savory juices of the food being cooked, giving it a flavor bonus. This is particularly true when poultry and meat are stuffed.

Another important function of a stuffing is to help retain the shape of food. In poultry it results in a plump, well-rounded bird even after roasting. In rolled meat and stuffed vegetable cups, stuffings help maintain the original shape.

Bread and rice are natural extenders for meat and poultry dishes. The starchy foods frequently used, such as bread, rice, pasta, and potatoes, almost eliminate the need for incorporating other high carbohydrate foods of this type in a well-balanced menu. For example, meat chops turn into hearty servings when stuffed with bread or rice. When mixed with poultry in a casserole, stuffing mixtures can turn the lowly casserole into an elegant entrée for luncheon or dinner.

Stuffed Pork Chops

Have the meat market cut pockets in each thick pork chop for easy stuffing—

6 pork chops, 1¼ to 1½ inches
    thick (3½ to 4 pounds)
Salt
Pepper

• • •

1½ cups toasted bread cubes
½ cup chopped, unpeeled apple
2 ounces sharp natural Cheddar
    cheese, shredded (½ cup)
2 tablespoons light raisins

• • •

2 tablespoons butter or margarine,
    melted
2 tablespoons orange juice
¼ teaspoon salt
⅛ teaspoon ground cinnamon

Have a pocket cut in each chop along the fat side. Salt and pepper inside of pockets. Toss together bread cubes, apple, cheese, and raisins. Combine melted butter, orange juice, salt, and cinnamon; pour over bread-fruit mixture and mix gently. Stuff pork chops lightly. Place in a shallow baking pan. Bake at 350° for 1¼ hours. Cover lightly with foil; bake about 15 minutes more. Makes 6 servings.

Stuff poultry lightly. First, fill and close neck cavity. Then, place bird, neck end down, in a large bowl; lightly spoon in stuffing.

Chicken-Dressing Bake

1 7- or 8-ounce package herb-
    seasoned stuffing mix
1 10½-ounce can condensed cream
    of mushroom soup
2 cups chicken broth
2 well-beaten eggs

• • •

2½ cups diced, cooked chicken *or*
    turkey
½ cup milk
2 tablespoons chopped, canned
    pimiento

Toss stuffing mix with *half* can of the soup, the chicken broth, and beaten eggs. Spread mixture in 11 x 7 x 1½-inch baking pan. Top with the cooked chicken or turkey. Combine remaining half can of soup with milk and pimiento; pour over all. Cover with foil. Bake at 350° till set, about 45 minutes. Serves 6 to 8.

The nutritional value of stuffing depends on the major ingredients of the mixture. If it is a bread, rice, or potato stuffing, it will add primarily carbohydrate to the diet. In addition, stuffings baked inside of poultry cavities will also contribute fat to the diet. If you are

Close cavity by holding skin together with pins or skewers; lace closed. Or tie legs to tail or tuck under band of skin at tail.

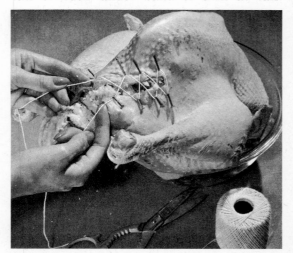

counting calories, a good way to cut down the amount of fat in a stuffing is to bake it separately in a casserole. By doing this, the drippings from the meat are not absorbed by the stuffing.

Types of stuffings

Dividing stuffings into types is an arbitrary way of grouping them because the categories frequently overlap. For example, bread stuffings occasionally contain some fruit or cooked meat, but that doesn't necessarily make them a fruit or meat stuffing. Or, vegetable or fruit stuffings frequently contain bread, but they aren't always considered bread stuffings. The main types can be classified by their basic ingredients — starchy stuffings, those made with meat or seafood, and stuffings made with fruit or vegetables.

Stuffing made with starchy foods: This is perhaps the most commonly used type of stuffing for meat, poultry, or fish. It is made with bread, cooked rice, dried peas or beans, or potatoes as the base, then seasoned with a variety of herbs.

There is disagreement as to whether bread stuffings should be moist or dry, and it's difficult to win an adherent of

Choose thick or double rib pork chops for stuffing. Stuffing pocket should be cut along fat side. Lightly spoon in stuffing.

one type to the opposite view. What stuffing a person prefers is usually the kind he is accustomed to. Many recipes make allowance for this factor and suggest adding desired amount of liquid.

Stuffing made with meat or seafood: By adding meat such as sausage or bacon, or seafood such as oysters, a richer, heartier stuffing mixture is obtained. This type is especially good for dry, white-meated poultry, lean cuts of meat, or lean types of fish. Other uses for meaty stuffings include green peppers and cabbage leaves stuffed with a mixture of ground meat.

Stuffing made with fruits or vegetables: This type of stuffing, composed mainly of fruit or vegetable ingredients, is often used when stuffing fish or poultry. Apples and oranges are favorite fruits with fish and poultry, while corn is a popular vegetable stuffing. Restuffed vegetables such as twice-baked potatoes are another version of a vegetable stuffing.

Basic preparation

All stuffings are built on some base ingredient. Bread is the most common type of base, whether it's in crumbs or small cubes. Dry bread makes the best stuffing. If you don't have dried bread, you can dry some fresh bread in the oven.

Although white bread is the most familiar type, it is not the only one used in stuffings. For example, Southerners prefer a stuffing made with corn bread. In addition, packaged stuffing mixes and croutons, which eliminate some preparation steps, are frequently used. Just follow package directions when preparing these convenience products.

Rice is another popular base ingredient for stuffings. Choose from long-grain rice or the quicker-cooking varieties. Brown rice is a flavorful variety. And for those special occasions, wild rice and wild rice mixes add an elegant touch.

Not as commonly known are stuffings using potatoes, either sweet or white. Dry beans can also be used as the base for a stuffing. The following recipe starts out with dried navy beans.

Sausage-Bean Stuffing Supreme

In a large saucepan combine 4 cups water, 1 cup small, dry navy beans (8 ounces), and 2 chicken bouillon cubes. Bring to boiling and boil gently for about 2 minutes. Remove from heat; cover and let stand 1 hour.

Add 8 ounces pork sausage links, cut in bite-sized pieces; 1 medium tomato, peeled and chopped; ½ cup finely chopped onion; ¼ cup finely chopped celery; ¼ cup snipped parsley; 1 small clove garlic, minced; ½ teaspoon dried thyme leaves, crushed; 1 small bay leaf; and ¼ teaspoon salt. Return to boiling; cover and simmer for about 1 hour. Stir in ¼ cup dry white wine. Boil gently, uncovered, till liquid is absorbed, about 30 minutes. Makes 4 cups.

Seasonings are also an important part of stuffings. Salt and pepper are musts with most recipes, and sage often finds its way into poultry bread stuffings. Other herbs frequently used in stuffings include rosemary, savory, marjoram, and thyme. Occasionally, ground spices are added to fruit stuffings for extra flavor.

Fat of some type is incorporated into dressings for additional richness. Not only is melted butter or margarine used, but bacon drippings are sometimes used along with the cooked bacon pieces. Cooked sausage also contributes fat.

Most dressings also need some additional moisture, whether it's in the form of eggs, water, milk, broth, fruit or vege-

Stuff a pair of broiler-fryer chickens with a sweet potato-apple mixture. Then, garnish Roast Chicken with Stuffing with crab apples and lots of parsley. (See *Roaster* for recipe.)

table juices, or chopped fruits or vegetables. Canned soups are another possible addition. The drippings from the cooking poultry or meat also make a flavorful contribution to the moistness of a stuffing.

In addition to these basic ingredients, other foods also enhance the flavor. Chopped vegetables, onion, garlic, and celery cooked in butter are frequent additions. Olives, mushrooms, apples, raisins, chestnuts and other nuts, oysters, clams, and giblets are other favorites.

How to use

With all the ingredients combined lightly together, you are ready to stuff the prepared poultry, meat, fish, or vegetables. (See *Game* and *Poultry* for complete roasting directions.) If all the stuffing doesn't fit in the cavity you are filling, bake the extra in a covered, greased casserole the last 30 to 60 minutes. If desired, baste mixture with pan drippings.

In poultry: Be sure to stuff all types of poultry—turkey, chicken, duck, goose, and Cornish game hens—just before cooking. It is not advisable to refrigerate the stuffed uncooked bird because there is too much chance of bacterial contamination. In addition, turkeys should not be stuffed and then frozen under home conditions for the same reasons of safety.

Commercially frozen stuffed turkeys, on the other hand, are perfectly safe to eat because these turkeys are frozen at temperatures well below zero degrees with constantly moving cold air. Commercial processes and techniques are difficult to duplicate in the home kitchen.

When you stuff poultry, use a light hand and don't tightly pack the mixture into the cavity of the bird. This is especially important for bread stuffings. The stuffing expands when it is cooked. If the bird is overstuffed, the dressing may become soggy and solid or compact.

At the end of the meal, remove any leftover stuffing from the cavities of poultry for the same reason that poultry is not to be stuffed ahead of time—bacteria. Store leftover stuffing promptly in a covered container in the refrigerator.

How Much Stuffing For Poultry

The following amounts of stuffing are based on approximately ¾ cup of stuffing per pound of ready-to-cook poultry. Amounts may vary, however, depending on the type of stuffing used. If packaged mixes are used, follow label directions.

Ready-to-cook weight	Amount of stuffing
2 to 4 pounds	1½ to 3 cups
4½ to 8 pounds	3½ to 6 cups
8½ to 12 pounds	6½ to 9 cups
12½ to 16 pounds	9½ to 12 cups
16½ to 20 pounds	12½ to 15 cups
20½ to 24 pounds	15½ to 18 cups

Bread Stuffing

     3 tablespoons chopped onion
    ¼ cup butter or margarine
           •   •   •
     4 cups dry bread cubes (about
         7 slices, cut in ½-inch cubes)
    ½ teaspoon poultry seasoning
    ½ teaspoon ground sage
    ¼ teaspoon salt
    ¼ teaspoon pepper
     2 to 4 tablespoons water *or*
         chicken broth

Cook onion in butter. Combine with bread, poultry seasoning, sage, salt, and pepper. Toss with enough liquid to moisten. Makes about 3 cups stuffing or enough for a 4-pound chicken. Double recipe for an 8-pound turkey.

Chestnut Stuffing: Cover 3 cups (1 pound) fresh chestnuts in shells with water; simmer 15 minutes. Drain. Make gash in shells with sharp knife; peel off shells while the nuts are still warm. Chop the chestnuts.

Prepare Bread Stuffing, cooking 1 cup chopped celery with the onion in 6 tablespoons butter or margarine. Add the chestnuts. Increase the salt to 1 teaspoon, and use ¼ cup turkey or chicken broth as the liquid.

Mushroom Stuffing: Prepare Bread Stuffing, adding one 6-ounce can sliced mushrooms, drained, *or* 1 cup sliced, fresh mushrooms cooked in a small amount of butter; toss.

Seafood Stuffing

Bake in a casserole or stuff a large chicken—

    4 cups dry bread cubes
    ¼ cup snipped parsley
    ½ teaspoon ground sage
    ¼ teaspoon dried thyme leaves,
        crushed
    ¼ teaspoon pepper
    ½ cup chopped celery
    ½ cup chopped onion
    2 tablespoons butter or margarine
        • • •
    1 10-ounce can frozen condensed
        cream of shrimp soup, thawed
    1 7½-ounce can crab meat,
        drained, flaked, and
        cartilage removed
    ¼ cup milk
    2 beaten eggs

Combine bread cubes, parsley, sage, thyme, and pepper. Cook celery and onion in butter or margarine till tender but not brown. Pour over bread in large bowl. Combine condensed soup, flaked crab meat, milk, and beaten eggs. Add to stuffing mixture and toss lightly till they are mixed. Makes about 5 cups stuffing.

Crab and shrimp soup give Seafood Stuffing special flavor. Stuffing that doesn't fit into the bird's cavities bakes separately.

Herb Stuffing

    12 cups slightly dry bread cubes
    ⅓ cup snipped parsley
    ⅓ cup finely chopped onion
    1½ teaspoons salt
    1 teaspoon ground sage
    1 teaspoon dried thyme leaves,
        crushed
    1 teaspoon dried rosemary leaves,
        crushed
    6 tablespoons butter, melted
    1 cup chicken broth

Combine all ingredients except broth. Add broth; toss lightly to mix. Makes about 8 cups.

Three Fruit Stuffing

    2 cups toasted bread cubes
    2 medium oranges, sectioned and
        diced (½ cup)
    1 small apple, peeled, cored, and
        chopped (½ cup)
    ¼ cup light raisins
    ¼ cup chopped pecans
    ½ teaspoon salt
    ¼ teaspoon ground nutmeg

In large mixing bowl toss together all ingredients. Cover and let stand 1 hour. Stir before stuffing bird. Makes enough stuffing for one 4- or 5-pound duckling or chicken.

Orange Stuffing

Flavors blend well with duckling—

    2 cups finely diced celery
    ¼ cup butter or margarine, melted
    3 cups toasted bread cubes
    1 teaspoon grated orange peel
    ⅔ cup diced orange sections
        (2 medium oranges)
    ½ teaspoon salt
    ½ teaspoon poultry seasoning
    1 beaten egg

Cook celery in butter or margarine till tender but not brown. Add the remaining ingredients and dash pepper; toss lightly. Makes enough stuffing for a 5-pound duckling.

Corn Bread Stuffing

    8 to 10 slices bacon
    1 cup chopped celery
    ¼ cup chopped onion
    ½ cup water
    3 cups coarse corn bread crumbs
    6 slices toasted bread, cubed
    ½ teaspoon rubbed sage
    1 cup chicken *or* turkey broth

In skillet cook bacon till crisp; drain, reserving ¼ cup drippings. Crumble bacon and set aside. To skillet add celery, onion, and water. Cover and cook till barely tender, about 7 minutes. Combine bacon, reserved drippings, vegetable mixture, corn bread crumbs, toast crumbs, sage, and broth; toss well.

Bake, covered, in a 1½-quart casserole at 350° for 30 minutes. Makes 8 servings or enough stuffing for an 8-pound turkey.

Ground Beef Stuffing

    1 7-ounce package herb-seasoned
        stuffing croutons
    1 cup diced celery
    1 cup diced carrot
    ½ cup chopped onion
    3 tablespoons butter or margarine
    ½ pound ground beef
    2½ cups diced, peeled apple

Combine stuffing mix, 1 cup water, and ½ teaspoon salt. Cook celery, carrot, and onion in butter till almost tender. Add meat and ½ teaspoon salt; brown meat, breaking it into small pieces. Add to stuffing mix along with apples; toss to mix. Makes 8 cups stuffing or enough to stuff a 10- to 12-pound turkey.

Mincemeat Stuffing

Combine 1 cup prepared mincemeat, ¼ cup melted butter or margarine, and one 7- or 8-ounce package herb-seasoned stuffing mix. Add ¾ cup hot water to moisten; toss mixture lightly. Makes enough stuffing for one 3- to 4-pound chicken. Or stuffing may be baked in a covered, greased 1-quart casserole at 375° about 30 minutes. Add ¼ cup additional liquid when stuffing is baked in the casserole.

Italian Stuffing

    3 cups fine dry bread crumbs
    ½ cup grated Parmesan cheese
    ¼ cup snipped parsley
    2 teaspoons poultry seasoning
    ½ teaspoon salt
    ½ teaspoon pepper
        • • •
    1 cup chopped onion
    ⅔ cup chopped celery
    1 large clove garlic, minced
    ½ cup butter or margarine
        Turkey or chicken giblets, cooked,
            drained (reserve ⅔ to 1 cup
            broth), and chopped
    1 10-ounce package frozen, chopped
        spinach, cooked and drained
    2 beaten eggs

Combine first 6 ingredients. Cook onion, celery, and garlic in butter till tender. Add to bread mixture along with remaining ingredients and broth. Toss lightly. Makes 8 cups or enough stuffing for 10- to 12-pound turkey.

French Bread Stuffing

Combine 8 cups French bread cubes, 1 cup coarse cracker crumbs, and 1 teaspoon ground sage. Cook 1 cup chopped onion and ½ cup finely chopped celery in ½ cup butter or margarine till vegetables are tender; pour over bread mixture. Add one 10½-ounce can condensed cream of chicken soup, 2 beaten eggs, and ¼ cup snipped parsley; toss the mixture lightly to mix. Makes about 6 cups, or enough for an 8-pound turkey or two 4-pound chickens.

Sesame-Rice Stuffing

An elegant stuffing for Cornish game hens—

Cook ⅓ cup chopped celery in 2 tablespoons butter or margarine till tender but not brown. Mix in 3 tablespoons sesame seed, toasted; 1 tablespoon dried onion flakes; 1 tablespoon dried parsley flakes; ½ teaspoon salt; and dash dried thyme leaves, crushed. Combine with 2 cups cooked long-grain rice, tossing lightly till mixed. Makes about 2 cups rice stuffing or enough for four Cornish game hens.

Holiday Rice Stuffing

Melt 2 tablespoons butter in a saucepan; cook ½ cup chopped green onions, ½ cup chopped parsley, and 1 cup grated carrots in butter for 10 minutes, stirring frequently. Add 1 cup uncooked long-grain rice and stir till well mixed; add 3 cups chicken broth, ½ teaspoon salt, and dash pepper. Cook, covered, over low heat till the rice is done, about 20 minutes. Makes enough stuffing for two chickens.

Pineapple-Stuffed Cornish Hens

　4　1-pound ready-to-cook Cornish game hens
　1　20½-ounce can pineapple chunks, drained
　1　teaspoon salt
　½　cup butter or margarine, melted
　2　tablespoons lemon juice

Rinse birds; pat dry with paper toweling. Lightly salt cavities. Stuff birds with pineapple. Truss the birds and tie the cavities closed. Mount crosswise on spit, alternating front-back, front-back. Do not have birds touching. Secure with extra-long holding forks. Combine salt, butter, and lemon juice; brush birds with mixture. Place on rotisserie over *medium* coals. Broil till done, about 1 to 1¼ hours, brushing birds with lemon butter every 15 minutes. Makes 4 servings.

In meat: Bread, rice, and vegetable stuffings pair well, flavorwise, with meats of all types and cuts. Cheese is a popular flavor addition for stuffed meat roasts and chops and so are herbs.

When planning family menus, vary everyday meatballs by wrapping ground meat around stuffing for a surprise center. Or, roll up a ground meat mixture with a stuffing, jelly-roll fashion.

A main dish version of a jelly roll

← Pat the ground meat mixture for Filled Beef Roll on a sheet of waxed paper. Spread rice mixture on meat and roll like a jelly roll.

Filled Beef Roll

　1　beaten egg
　¼　cup milk
　½　cup finely crushed saltine cracker crumbs (14 crackers)
　¼　cup chopped onion
　½　teaspoon salt
　　　Dash pepper
　1　pound ground beef
　1　cup cooked rice
　2　ounces process Swiss cheese, shredded (½ cup)
　2　tablespoons chopped green pepper

Combine first 6 ingredients. Add beef; mix well. On a piece of waxed paper, pat mixture into a 10x8-inch rectangle. Combine cooked rice, cheese, and green pepper. Pat onto meat, leaving a 1-inch margin around edge. Roll jelly-roll fashion, beginning with narrow side. Seal side seam and ends. Place roll, seam side down, in 11x7x1½-inch baking pan. Bake at 350° for 35 minutes. Let stand 5 minutes before serving. Makes 4 or 5 servings.

Stuffed Rolled Rib Roast

　¼　cup chopped onion
　1　clove garlic, minced
　1　tablespoon brown sugar
　1　teaspoon salt
　　　Dash pepper
　1　teaspoon prepared mustard
　1　teaspoon Worcestershire sauce
　1　cup soft bread crumbs
　1　3- to 4-pound rolled beef rib roast
　1　3-ounce can sliced mushrooms, drained
　2　tablespoons chopped pimiento-stuffed green olives
　2　ounces sharp process American cheese, shredded (½ cup)

Combine first 8 ingredients and ¼ cup water. Unroll roast. Spread with bread mixture; sprinkle with mushrooms, olives, and cheese. Reroll roast and tie securely; fasten ends with skewers. Place on rack in shallow pan. Roast at 325° to desired doneness (1½ to 2 hours for rare, 1¾ to 2¼ hours for medium, or 2 to 2½ hours for well-done). Serves 9 to 12.

Stuffed Beef Round

Using a 2-pound beef round steak, cut ½ inch thick, cut meat into 6 serving-sized pieces. Pound to ¼-inch thickness. Combine 4 ounces sharp process American cheese, shredded (1 cup); ½ cup *each* chopped onion and chopped celery; and ¼ cup snipped parsley. Place about ¼ *cup* cheese mixture in center of each piece of steak, reserving remaining cheese mixture (about 1 cup). Roll up each steak jelly-roll fashion; secure with wooden picks.

Combine ¼ cup all-purpose flour, 1 teaspoon salt, and ⅛ teaspoon pepper. Roll meat in flour mixture to coat. In skillet slowly brown meat in 2 tablespoons salad oil. Drain off excess fat. Combine one 10½-ounce can condensed beef broth and ½ teaspoon dry mustard; add to steak rolls. Cover; simmer 45 minutes.

Add reserved cheese mixture to skillet; simmer till meat is tender, 15 to 30 minutes more. Remove meat to heated platter. Skim excess fat from pan juices. Blend together 2 tablespoons all-purpose flour and ¼ cup water; stir into pan juices. Cook, stirring constantly, till sauce thickens and bubbles. Pour over meat rolls. Makes 6 servings.

Roast Stuffed Lamb

Have a 4- to 5-pound lamb shoulder roast boned, forming a pocket. Cook 1 cup chopped celery and ¼ cup chopped onion in ¼ cup butter or margarine till tender. Toss with 6 cups soft bread crumbs (about 9 slices), ½ cup apricot nectar, 2 beaten eggs, 2 teaspoons poultry seasoning, and 1 teaspoon salt. Fill pocket of roast with stuffing; skewer securely.

Place roast on rack in shallow pan. Bake at 325° till meat thermometer registers 175° to 180°, about 3 to 3¾ hours. Remove strings and skewers before serving. Makes 8 servings.

In fish: One way to prepare either large dressed fish or smaller pan-dressed fish is by stuffing and baking. The stuffing not only adds flavor but enhances the appearance of the finished fish.

Since fish have a comparatively smaller cavity than poultry, less stuffing is needed per pound of fish. This is a good time to bake any extra stuffing separately.

Corn-Stuffed Whitefish

    1 3-pound fresh or frozen, dressed
        whitefish or other fish, boned
    ¼ cup chopped onion
    3 tablespoons chopped green
        pepper
    1 tablespoon butter or margarine
    1 12-ounce can whole kernel corn,
        drained
    1 cup soft bread crumbs
        (1½ slices)
    2 tablespoons chopped, canned
        pimiento
    ⅛ teaspoon dried thyme leaves,
        crushed
    2 tablespoons salad oil

Thaw frozen fish; dry fish. Sprinkle inside generously with salt. Place fish in well-greased shallow baking pan. In saucepan cook onion and green pepper in butter till tender. Stir in corn, crumbs, pimiento, ½ teaspoon salt, and thyme. Stuff fish loosely with mixture. Brush fish generously with oil; cover with foil. Bake at 350° till fish flakes easily when tested with a fork, 45 to 60 minutes. Remove to serving platter, using two spatulas. Serves 6.

Luau Fish Bake

Use one 2-pound fresh or frozen, dressed trout or other fish, boned. Thaw frozen fish. Season fish cavity with salt. Brush with lemon juice. In small saucepan cook ¼ cup diced celery, ¼ cup chopped green pepper, and 2 tablespoons chopped onion in 3 tablespoons butter till tender. Toss with 1½ cups herb-seasoned stuffing mix and 3 tablespoons water.

Place fish on greased heavy foil; stuff cavity. Brush with ¼ cup bottled barbecue sauce. Seal foil. Place in shallow baking pan. Bake at 350° for 45 minutes. Turn back foil. Bake till fish tests done, about 15 minutes. Brush with ¼ cup bottled barbecue sauce. Serves 4.

A prize catch

To save time when preparing Corn-Stuffed →
Whitefish, use canned corn with peppers and
omit pepper and pimiento from ingredients.

In vegetables: Stuffed vegetables are a natural dish in almost every cuisine. Popular American favorites are stuffed peppers, squash, and potatoes. Stuffed tomatoes are a variation of stuffed peppers.

Stuffed cabbage leaves, although originally a foreign dish, have become an American favorite. Most often, the individual leaves are stuffed, but occasionally the entire cabbage is stuffed.

Deviled-Stuffed Potatoes

Bake 4 large baking potatoes at 425° till done, about 45 to 50 minutes. Cut slice from top of each. Scoop out inside; mash. Add ¼ cup softened butter, ½ teaspoon salt, ½ teaspoon prepared mustard, and ⅛ teaspoon paprika. Beat in enough hot milk to make stiff consistency (about ½ cup). Stir in one 4½-ounce can deviled ham, just enough to swirl meat through potatoes. Pile mixture back into potato shells. Return to oven. Bake till heated through and lightly browned, about 20 minutes. Serves 4.

Sausage-Stuffed Squash

  3 medium acorn squash
  1 pound bulk pork sausage
  ¼ cup chopped green pepper
  ¼ cup chopped onion
  1 1½-ounce envelope cheese sauce
      mix
  1 3-ounce can chopped mushrooms
  ½ cup fine dry bread crumbs
  1 tablespoon butter, melted

Cut squash in half lengthwise; remove seeds. Bake, cut side down, in shallow pan at 350° till tender, 35 to 40 minutes.

Meanwhile, in skillet cook sausage with green pepper and onion till meat is brown and vegetables are crisp-tender. Drain off excess fat. Blend sauce mix with meat. Add liquid following package directions. Cook and stir till thickened and bubbly. Drain mushrooms and stir into the sausage mixture.

Fill the squash cavities with the sausage mixture. Combine bread crumbs with melted butter. Sprinkle atop the squash. Continue baking till the crumbs are lightly browned, about 15 to 20 minutes. Makes 6 servings.

Saucy Cabbage Rolls

  6 large cabbage leaves
  1 beaten egg
  ½ cup milk
  ¾ cup cooked long-grain rice
  ½ teaspoon salt
  ¼ teaspoon dried dillweed
  ⅛ teaspoon pepper
  1 pound ground beef
  1 10½-ounce can mushroom gravy
  ¼ cup catsup
  ⅓ cup finely chopped onion
  ¼ teaspoon dried dillweed

Immerse cabbage leaves (heavy center vein of leaf may be cut out about 2 inches) in boiling water just till limp, about 3 minutes; drain. Combine egg, milk, cooked rice, salt, ¼ teaspoon dillweed, and pepper. Add beef; mix well. Place about ½ cup meat mixture in center of each cabbage leaf; fold in the sides of leaves and roll the ends over meat.

In skillet combine remaining ingredients and ⅓ cup water. Add cabbage rolls. Cover and cook over low heat 30 minutes, stirring occasionally. Uncover and cook 15 minutes longer, stirring occasionally. Makes 6 servings.

Stuffed Tomato Cups

Cut tops off 4 large tomatoes; scoop out pulp. Chop tops and pulp; drain. Cut sawtooth edges around shells; drain. Sprinkle inside of shell with salt and dried basil leaves, crushed.

In skillet brown ½ pound ground beef with ¼ cup chopped onion; drain. Stir in tomato pulp, ⅔ cup herb-seasoned stuffing croutons, ½ teaspoon salt, and ¼ teaspoon Worcestershire sauce. Stuff shells with mixture.

Sprinkle *each* tomato with 1 teaspoon grated Parmesan cheese. Place in shallow baking dish. Fill dish with ½ inch water. Bake at 375° for 25 to 30 minutes. Remove from water. Trim with parsley, if desired. Makes 4 servings.

Variation of stuffed peppers

A seasoned mixture of ground beef and stuffing croutons are baked in sawtooth-edged Stuffed Tomato Cups—a one-dish meal. →

STURGEON *(stûr' juhn)* — A large, saltwater and freshwater fish that is prized for its flesh, eggs, and isinglass. Sturgeon live in the waters of Europe, Asia, and North America. Some live along the seacoasts and go into the rivers to spawn; others stay in the rivers all their lives.

The flesh of the sturgeon is dry and quite similar to the meat of tuna. When smoked, sturgeon has a delicate flavor that needs little seasoning. The eggs of the female are highly prized as the base for caviar. Another valued product of sturgeon is isinglass, a gelatin from the air bladder used in glues and jellies, and as a clarifier in some products.

The nutritive value of sturgeon comes from its high-quality protein. There are 160 calories in a 3½-ounce serving of fresh fish that is steamed, while a 3½-ounce serving of smoked sturgeon adds 149 calories to the diet. (See also *Fish.*)

SUBMARINE SANDWICH — Another name for the hero, hoagy, or poor boy sandwich. It is made with rolls or a loaf of bread, split lengthwise, and filled with meat, fish, cheese, lettuce, and relishes. (See also *Poor Boy Sandwich.*)

Submarine Sandwich

Brown a giant brown-and-serve French roll (about 8 inches long) according to package directions. Split roll lengthwise, *but don't cut quite through.* Scoop out some of center. Spread generously with prepared mustard, garlic butter, and/or mayonnaise mixed with curry powder. Line bottom of roll with leaf lettuce. Pile on slices of corned beef, boiled ham, bologna, salami, pickled tongue, chicken, tuna, and herring as desired. Add slices of American and Swiss cheese, onion, green and ripe olives, and dill pickle. Anchor sandwich with wooden picks. Makes 1 generous serving.

SUBSTITUTIONS — The replacement of ingredients with other ingredients to produce similar characteristics. In most recipes, alternate ingredients can be used with satisfactory results. Common substitutions are listed in the next column.

Emergency substitutions

1 cup sifted cake flour = 1 cup minus 2 tablespoons sifted all-purpose flour

1 tablespoon cornstarch (for thickening) = 2 tablespoons flour or 4 teaspoons quick-cooking tapioca

1 teaspoon baking powder = ¼ teaspoon baking soda plus ½ cup buttermilk or sour milk (to replace ½ cup of liquid in recipe)

1 cup honey = 1¼ cups sugar plus ¼ cup liquid

1 cake compressed yeast = 1 package or 2 teaspoons active dry yeast

1 cup whole milk = ½ cup evaporated milk plus ½ cup water or 1 cup reconstituted nonfat dry milk plus 2½ teaspoons butter

1 cup sour milk or buttermilk = 1 tablespoon lemon juice or vinegar plus enough sweet milk to make 1 cup (let stand 5 minutes)

1 whole egg = 2 egg yolks (for use in custards)

1 square (1 ounce) unsweetened chocolate = 3 tablespoons unsweetened cocoa powder plus 1 tablespoon butter or margarine

1 tablespoon fresh snipped herbs = 1 teaspoon dried herbs

1 small fresh onion = 1 tablespoon instant minced onion, rehydrated

1 teaspoon dry mustard = 1 tablespoon prepared mustard

1 clove garlic = ⅛ teaspoon garlic powder

1 cup tomato juice = ½ cup tomato sauce plus ½ cup water

1 cup catsup or chili sauce = 1 cup tomato sauce plus ½ cup sugar and 2 tablespoons vinegar (for use in cooked mixtures)

In a few recipes, if you substitute one ingredient for another, even though of similar flavor, the product will be a failure. An example of this is chocolate angel food cake. If you substitute melted chocolate for the dry cocoa in the recipe, the fat in the chocolate will cause the egg white foam to break down and the cake won't rise properly. More often than not, however, one basic ingredient can be substituted for another.

SUCCOTASH *(suk' uh tash')*—A cooked vegetable dish made of sweet corn and beans, frequently limas. Sometimes green beans are used in combination with the corn. The name of the dish is derived from an American Indian word meaning pieces or fragments. Frozen and canned succotash mixtures are also available.

Succotash

Combine one 16-ounce can limas, drained; one 12-ounce can whole kernel corn, drained; 2 tablespoons butter or margarine; and ½ cup light cream. Heat through. Season to taste with salt and pepper. Makes 6 servings.

Savory Succotash

  1 16-ounce can French-style green beans, drained
  1 16-ounce can whole kernel corn, drained
½ cup mayonnaise or salad dressing
  2 ounces sharp process American cheese, shredded (½ cup)
½ cup chopped green pepper
½ cup chopped celery
  2 tablespoons chopped onion
  1 cup soft bread crumbs
  2 tablespoons butter, melted

Combine green beans, corn, mayonnaise, cheese, green pepper, celery, and onion. Turn mixture into a 10x6x1¾-inch baking dish. Combine soft bread crumbs and melted butter. Sprinkle crumb mixture atop casserole. Bake at 350° till crumbs are toasted and mixture is heated through, about 30 minutes. Serves 6.

Bean Succotash

¼ cup chopped onion
¼ cup chopped green pepper
  2 tablespoons butter or margarine
  1 16-ounce can French-style green beans, drained
  1 12-ounce can whole kernel corn, drained

Cook onion and green pepper in butter till tender. Add beans and corn. Season to taste with salt and pepper. Cover; heat. Garnish with green pepper rings, if desired. Serves 6.

SUCKER—**1.** A freshwater fish of North America that lives in rivers and ponds. This fish is not prized as a catch, especially in the summer when its flesh is soft and tasteless. **2.** A hard candy eaten off of a stick, also called lollipop.

SUCKLING PIG—A young pig, with delicate flesh, that is still nursing. The pig is generally roasted whole. (See also *Pork.*)

SUET *(soo' it)*—The solid, white fat from the loin and kidney regions of meat animals. Beef suet is the kind most often used for larding meat or in steamed puddings.

Bean Succotash, made with green beans, onion, and green pepper, is a variation of the traditional lima-corn vegetable dish.

SUGAR

*An everyday ingredient that is as important today
as it was several hundred years ago.*

Sweets are easily the most favored of all foods. Scrumptious mouthfuls of desserts, candies, and pies delight the smallest child and adults of all ages. Considering the popularity of foods sweetened with sugar, it may come as quite a surprise to learn that sugar has been an important part in the diet of the Western World only within the last few centuries. Prior to that time, the cook relied on honey to bring out the sweetness of foods.

The modern-day reliance on sugar as a sweetener is bound up in the history of sugarcane, the long, slender cane that was chanced upon in New Guinea about 8,000 years ago. It took a long time for Western man to realize the value of sugar in his diet. Along the way, man carried the cane northward from the South Pacific to southeast Asia and India where sugar was in vogue before 400 B.C. Historians tell us that the army of Alexander the Great gained an acquaintance with sugar during a campaign in India in 325 B.C. As the years rolled by, sugar followed the early trade routes and battlefields from Asia to the Mediterranean, Europe, and later to America.

Economics has also played a major role in directing the course of the sugar industry. By the early nineteenth century, sugar was a basic commodity in Europe. Unfortunately for Napoleon I of France, the sugar trade was controlled by the British and the Emperor had to look else-where for the sweetener. Believing in all things French, Napoleon offered a reward to anyone who could produce sugar from locally grown crops. And this is where sugar prepared from the sugar beet entered the sweetening business.

Prior to Napoleon's interest in sugar-beet growing, a German chemist, Andreas Marggraf, in 1747 had proven that sugar could be produced from beets and that it was similar to the sugar from cane. This knowledge and Napoleon's influence brought about the introduction of sugar beets as part of the sugar industry.

Settlers in America used sugar beets to make farming profitable in many areas. The first factory using the beets was established on the East Coast in the 1830s, but this venture was unsuccessful. Later settlers in the central and far western United States also planted sugar beets and established the first profitable beet factory, built in 1870 in California.

This sugar beet production was in addition to the large plantings of sugarcane in the South, where it had been a familiar crop for many years — since it was first introduced into Louisiana in 1751.

Today, although the production of sugar from cane leads the production of sugar from beets by a ratio of about three to one, the United States is the second largest producer of beet sugar in the world.

Sugar, the familiar crystalline sweetener, is technically a carbohydrate known as sucrose and it comes primarily from sugarcane and sugar beets. A small proportion of sucrose also comes from the maple tree, sorghum cane, and certain palms, such as the wild date palm. Sucrose is related to other sugars found abundantly in nature, such as lactose in milk; fructose in fruits; glucose and

Three-layered dessert

← The Chocolate Cheesecake Torte filling is sweetened with granulated sugar while the top is dusted with confectioners' sugar.

dextrose in fruits, honey, and some vegetables; and maltose in corn syrup and malt.

The sweetness of these natural sugars varies, with fructose being the sweetest and sucrose, the familiar cooking and table ingredient, being the second most sweet. It is interesting to note that the sweetening ability, appearance, and cooking results are equal, whether sucrose is obtained from sugarcane or sugar beets.

How sugar is produced: All green plants produce sugar in their leaves. Sunlight produces chemical energy when it reacts with the plant pigment. This energy combines water which the plant takes from the soil with carbon dioxide from the air to form plant sugars. Sucrose produced in this way is the same, whether it is formed in fruit, sugar beets, or sugarcane. What makes beets and cane more suited to sugar production is their capacity to store large amounts of sucrose.

Even though beets and cane produce the same kind of sugar, they are grown differently and many of the processes for making sugar from these sources differ.

Sugar from sugarcane: In the tropical and semitropical climates where sugarcane thrives, many harvests are made from the same rootstock. These rootstocks remain in the ground after cutting and send up new shoots each year. During the growing season, the plants may reach 18 feet in height. The cane is harvested either by a machine or with a machete.

The cut stalks are stripped of leaves and shipped to the sugar mill where they are crushed and shredded. The juice is extracted from the cane by forcing it through heavy rollers under pressure. The juice is purified, then boiled to concentrate the sugar. Further boiling in vacuum pans helps the sucrose to crystallize. At this point in processing, the product looks like a thick mass of crystals and liquid. The sugar is separated from the syrup in a machine with a rapid, spinning action. The sucrose crystals are trapped in a wire basket and the syrup spins on through to be returned for further refining. When refining is completed, the resulting molasses, known as blackstrap, a thick black syrup with a bitter flavor, also is sold.

The sugar at this stage of production is called raw sugar and in this form it is shipped to United States refineries from certain foreign countries. Sugarcane is also raised in Florida, Louisiana, and Hawaii, from which raw sugar is transported to cane refineries. At domestic refineries these further steps are then taken: 1. The raw sugar is rinsed to remove any molasses that clings to the crystals. The sugar is then dissolved in warm water. 2. The syrup is filtered several times to remove impurities and color. 3. The syrup is boiled to recrystallize the sugar. It is again separated in a spinning machine, dried, and packaged.

Sugar from sugar beets: Unlike the garden variety red beet, the sugar beet is silver-white and has a long, tapering shape. One beet weighs about two pounds and will produce about 14 teaspoons sugar. Sugar beets require a temperate climate in which to grow.

After harvest, sugar beets are shipped to the factory where they move along rapid streams of warm water. The beets are washed and sliced into thin strips similar in shape to shoestring potatoes. The sliced beets are soaked in large vats to extract the sugar. The thin syrup that results goes through a purification process of filtering. It is then boiled until it thickens and crystallizes.

As in the processing of cane sugar, a machine with a spinning action whirls the molasses away from the sugar. In American refineries, production does not stop at this raw sugar stage but continues until clean, fully refined sugar is obtained.

Nutritional value: The child just home from school and the office worker on his break both have found that a sweet snack restores vitality. The main contribution of sugar, a carbohydrate, is energy. The body begins to use sugar within five minutes after it is eaten; therefore, sugar is one of the fastest acting energy sources in the diet.

Despite its pep-giving potential, sugar has only about 45 calories per tablespoon. Of course, sweets, as well as higher calorie foods, need to be controlled when weight reduction is the goal.

Once the body is supplied with the needed vitamins, minerals, and proteins, there is still a need for energy-producing nutrients. At least half of our food intake contains carbohydrates. If carbohydrates are not sufficiently supplied in the diet, the body will use protein for energy. For this reason, sugar and other carbohydrates are said to have a protein-sparing effect. Remember, though, that calories consumed beyond need add pounds.

Types of sugar

There are several different types of sugar. Some types are used only commercially, but the majority can be purchased in the supermarket for use in the kitchen. Each kind has a familiar usage.

Granulated sugar: This is the white, refined sugar that comes from cane and beets. It is classed according to the size of the crystal. Fine sugar is used in the home for cooking and table service, and is the type most frequently purchased. Sugar is also available in cubes.

Extra-fine sugar is packaged for home cakemaking and for use in mixed drinks. Commercially, it is used for baking. Other forms—very-fine, medium-coarse, and coarse sugars—are for industrial use.

Confectioners' or powdered sugars: These pulverized sugars are used for icings, candies, and for dusting on finished products. Usually packed with small amounts of cornstarch to prevent caking, they are classified as ultra-fine (confectioners' 10X), very-fine (confectioners' 6X), fine (confectioners' 4X), medium, and coarse. Terminology varies.

Brown sugar: This is a fine crystal mass of partially refined sugar coated with a film of molasses-flavored syrup. Brown sugar adds flavor and color to recipes.

Brown sugar is available in three forms: light brown, dark brown, and granulated brown sugar. The lighter type of brown sugar is frequently used in baking and candymaking, while the richer flavor of the dark brown sugar is well suited to recipes such as gingerbread.

Maple sugar: This product comes from the sugar maple tree, rather than from beets or cane. It has a distinctive maple flavor and is delicious eaten as candy.

How to select and store

Sugars usually come in one-pound packages. Many also are available in two-pound units. Regular granulated sugar is packaged in 5-, 10-, and 25-pound bags as well because of its frequent use.

Some packages are suitable for storing sugar, but it is preferable to transfer sugar from paper bags into a container with a tight-fitting lid. Sugar can be stored on the shelf for up to a year.

Brown sugar that is purchased in a plastic bag may be stored in the bag, tightly closed. If you wish, empty the package into a container with a tight-fitting cover, then store in a cool, moist place. If the brown sugar should dry out, add a slice of apple to restore the moisture.

How to use

Sugar is more than simply a sweetener. It has properties that are essential to the structure, texture, and appearance of a great many recipes.

In baking: Sugar gives flavor, tenderness, and an even grain to such items as cakes, cookies, and breads, and contributes brownness during baking. In yeast breads, sugar speeds the growth of the yeast by providing it nourishment.

Sugar Cookies

Thoroughly cream 2/3 cup shortening, 3/4 cup sugar, and 1 teaspoon vanilla. Add 1 egg; beat till fluffy. Stir in 4 teaspoons milk. Sift together 2 cups sifted all-purpose flour, 1½ teaspoons baking powder, and ¼ teaspoon salt; blend into creamed mixture. Divide dough in half. Chill 1 hour. On lightly floured surface, roll ⅛ inch thick. Cut in desired shapes with cutters. Top with walnut half, if desired. Bake on greased cookie sheet at 375° for about 6 to 8 minutes. Cool slightly; remove cookies from pan. Makes 24 cookies.

Rhubaba

      3 tablespoons butter or margarine
    ½ cup brown sugar
    ½ pound rhubarb, diced (2 cups)
        Red food coloring
    ¼ cup dry sherry
      3 egg yolks
      1 teaspoon lemon juice
      1 cup granulated sugar
    ¼ cup hot water
      1 cup sifted all-purpose flour
    1½ teaspoons baking powder
    ¼ teaspoon salt
      3 stiff-beaten egg whites

Melt butter in a 9x2-inch round baking dish. Stir in the brown sugar. Remove from heat; top evenly with rhubarb. Add a few drops red food coloring to sherry; drizzle over rhubarb. In large mixer bowl beat egg yolks and lemon juice till thick and lemon-colored; gradually add the 1 cup sugar and beat till thick and light. Slowly stir in ¼ cup hot water.

Sift together the flour, baking powder, and salt. Add to the egg yolk mixture and mix just till well combined. Fold in beaten egg whites. Spoon batter evenly over rhubarb. Bake at 325° till cake tests done, about 1 hour. Remove from oven; let stand 5 minutes. Loosen sides and invert onto serving plate. Serve warm with whipped cream, if desired. Serves 6 to 8.

Sugar is so versatile that it can be used for an icing or coating on doughnuts or as an important ingredient in Sugar Cookies.

French Chocolate Coffee Cake

Combine 2 packages active dry yeast and 1½ cups sifted all-purpose flour. Combine ¾ cup sugar, ⅔ cup water, ½ cup butter, ⅓ cup evaporated milk, and ½ teaspoon salt. Heat just till warm; add to yeast mixture. Add 4 egg yolks. Beat at low speed ½ minute; beat 3 minutes at high speed. Stir in 2½ cups sifted all-purpose flour; blend well.

Place in greased bowl; turn once. Cover; let rise till double, 2 hours. Punch down; turn onto floured surface and let rest 10 minutes. Meanwhile, combine ¾ cup semisweet chocolate pieces, ⅓ cup evaporated milk, 2 tablespoons sugar, and ½ teaspoon ground cinnamon. Cook and stir the mixture over low heat till chocolate melts; cool.

Roll dough to an 18x10-inch rectangle. Spread with chocolate mixture; roll up from long side. Seal and join ends. Place seam side down in greased 10-inch tube pan.

Combine ¼ cup all-purpose flour, ¼ cup sugar, and 1 teaspoon ground cinnamon. Cut in ¼ cup butter or margarine. Stir in ¼ cup semisweet chocolate pieces and ¼ cup chopped nuts. Sprinkle on dough. Let rise till double, 1¼ hours. Bake at 350° about 50 minutes. Cool 15 minutes before removing from pan.

In range-top cooking: Starch mixtures benefit from the action of sugar, for it disperses the starch granules, preventing lumps. Dry starches, such as flour and cornstarch, should be mixed with the amount of sugar given in the recipe before adding the liquid. Softening gelatin in liquid can be eliminated by mixing gelatin with the sugar in the recipe.

Many nonsweet foods benefit from the addition of some sugar, too. Oversalting can be counteracted somewhat by adding a little sugar, and the flavor of an overly tart fruit such as rhubarb or sour cherries can be toned down with a little sugar.

Sugar also adds flavor to vegetables, main dishes, salad dressings, and soups. Some sugar in the cooking water restores the fresh flavor to vegetables, which begin to lose natural sugars as soon as they are picked. Some cooks sprinkle sugar on meats that are to be stewed or pot-roasted before the meat is browned. The sugar caramelizes and has a pleasant effect on both the color and flavor. Sweet-sour dishes owe their sweetness to sugar.

Spicy Peach Compote

   3 large, fresh peaches
   2 teaspoons cornstarch
   2 tablespoons sugar
  ½ of 6-ounce can pineapple-orange
      juice concentrate, thawed
      (⅓ cup)
  ½ teaspoon grated orange peel
   4 inches stick cinnamon
   5 whole cloves

Peel, halve, and pit peaches; sprinkle with ascorbic acid color keeper or lemon juice mixed with water to prevent darkening. In saucepan mix cornstarch, sugar, and ¼ teaspoon salt. Stir in concentrate, ⅔ cup water, peel, cinnamon, and cloves. Cook and stir till thickened and bubbly; cook and stir 2 minutes longer. Pour hot mixture over peaches; chill. Remove the spices before serving. Serves 6.

In candies and frostings: Sugar is the major ingredient of both candies and many types of frostings.

When making candy, the concentration of sugar, degree of heat, agitation, and other ingredients determine the types of candy. Most fall into two general types—crystalline and noncrystalline. The crystals in crystalline candy are too small to be felt on the tongue. Examples of crystalline candies include fudge, fondant, and divinity. The noncrystalline candies are cooked until very thick, then cooled quickly before crystallization takes place. Peanut brittle and caramels are examples.

Many frostings and other bread and cake toppings are prepared with different types of sugars. Confectioners' sugar is frequently used with other ingredients for uncooked frostings and icings. Alone, confectioners' sugar can be sifted over a cake for a decorative topping. Granulated sugar is often used in cooked frostings, such as seven-minute, boiled, and fudge frosting, while brown sugar is a favorite for broiled-on toppers.

Almond Caramels

   1 cup granulated sugar
  ½ cup brown sugar
  ½ cup light corn syrup
 1½ cups light cream
  ¼ cup butter or margarine
   1 teaspoon vanilla
  ½ cup chopped, toasted almonds

Butter bottom and sides of 9x5x3-inch loaf pan. In 2-quart saucepan combine sugars, corn syrup, cream, and ¼ cup butter. Cook and stir over medium heat till sugars dissolve. Continue cooking, stirring occasionally, to firm-ball stage (248°). Remove from heat; stir in vanilla and almonds. Turn into prepared pan; cool. Cut in squares; wrap each. Makes 36.

Lemon Butter Frosting

   6 tablespoons butter or margarine
   4 cups sifted confectioners' sugar
   1 egg yolk
 1½ teaspoons vanilla
   1 teaspoon grated lemon peel
   2 to 3 tablespoons light cream

Cream butter; gradually add *half* the confectioners' sugar, blending well. Beat in egg yolk, vanilla, and lemon peel. Add remaining confectioners' sugar; beat well. Add enough light cream to make of spreading consistency. Frosts two 8- or 9-inch layers.

Milk Chocolate Frosting

Blender makes sugar very fine—

   1 cup granulated sugar
   3 1-ounce squares unsweetened
      chocolate, cut in small pieces
   1 6-ounce can evaporated milk

Put sugar in blender; cover and blend about 1 minute at high speed. Add chocolate, evaporated milk, and dash salt; blend at high speed about 3 minutes or till thick, using rubber spatula to scrape sides as necessary when blender is turned off. Frosts tops of two 8-inch layers. (If a firmer frosting is desired, chill the frosted cake before serving.)

Quick Christmas Braid is simple to make. Thawed, frozen bread dough is rolled out and filled with a brown sugar mixture. After baking, confectioners' sugar icing is drizzled atop.

Quick Christmas Braid

A jiffy coffee bread with a brown sugar-cinnamon filling and confectioners' sugar icing—

1 16-ounce loaf frozen bread
    dough
2 tablespoons butter or margarine,
    softened
¼ cup brown sugar
½ teaspoon ground cinnamon
¼ cup chopped pecans
1 cup sifted confectioners' sugar
4 to 5 teaspoons milk
    Red sugar
    Pecan halves

Thaw frozen dough completely; roll to 12-inch square. Cut in 3 strips. Spread butter or margarine down lengthwise center of each strip. Combine brown sugar and cinnamon; sprinkle over butter. Top with chopped pecans.

Bring dough up around filling, sealing edges, to form three ropes. Place on greased baking sheet and loosely braid. Let rise till double, about 30 minutes. Bake at 375° for 30 to 35 minutes. (Cover braid with foil the last few minutes of baking if necessary to prevent over-browning.) Combine confectioners' sugar and enough milk to make a thin glaze. Drizzle over braid while it is still warm. Sprinkle the top of braid with red sugar and trim with the pecan halves. Makes 1 braid.

Chocolate Cheesecake Torte

Confectioners' sugar is sprinkled on top of cake—

- 1 package 2-layer-size German chocolate cake mix
- 1 11-ounce can mandarin orange sections
- 1 envelope unflavored gelatin (1 tablespoon)
- 1 8-ounce package cream cheese, softened
- 1 cup granulated sugar
- 2 egg yolks
- ½ teaspoon grated lemon peel
- 1 tablespoon lemon juice
- 2 egg whites
- ½ cup whipping cream
  Confectioners' sugar

Prepare cake mix according to package directions. Pour into two greased and floured 9x1½-inch round layer pans. Bake at 350° for 25 to 30 minutes. Cool 10 minutes. Remove from pans. Cool the cake layers thoroughly.

Drain oranges, reserving ¼ cup syrup. Dice sections; set aside. Soften gelatin in reserved syrup. Dissolve over hot water. Cool slightly. Beat together cream cheese and granulated sugar. Beat in egg yolks, lemon peel, and juice. Stir in cooled gelatin. Beat egg whites till stiff; whip cream. Fold egg whites and cream into gelatin mixture along with oranges. Turn into an 8x1½-inch round layer pan. Chill till set. Unmold onto bottom cake layer. Cover with second cake layer. Sift confectioners' sugar lightly over top of the cake.

Peanut Butter–Peach Cake

Drain one 16-ounce can sliced peaches, reserving ¼ cup syrup. In a saucepan combine ¼ cup butter, ⅓ cup peanut butter, ½ cup brown sugar, and reserved peach syrup. Cook over medium heat till ingredients are melted and blended. Pour into an 8x8x2-inch baking pan. Place peaches in rows over mixture.

Prepare 1 package 1-layer-size yellow cake mix according to package directions. Carefully pour over top of peaches. Bake at 350° till cake is done, about 50 minutes. Cool cake 5 minutes. Invert on cake plate. Serve plain or with whipped cream. Makes 9 servings.

In frozen desserts: Sugar improves the texture of ice cream and sherbet by hindering the formation of large ice crystals. The tiny ice crystals which form in the frozen mixture have a smooth and creamy feeling on the tongue.

In preserving: Sugar is used in producing a tender gel in jams, jellies, and other types of preserves. Fruits vary in sugar content, and so the amount of sugar added depends on the fruit used. Sugar also acts as a preservative in jellies and contributes to the flavor of the product.

Freezer Pineapple Conserve

- 1 large, fresh pineapple
- 1 teaspoon grated orange peel
- ½ cup orange juice
  Several drops yellow food coloring
- 5 cups sugar
- ½ cup chopped walnuts
- ½ cup flaked coconut
- 1 package powdered fruit pectin

Peel and core the pineapple; cut into pieces. Place pineapple, a few pieces at a time, in blender container; cover and blend on low speed till finely chopped (not puréed). Measure 2 cups chopped pineapple into a bowl. Add orange peel, orange juice, and food coloring. Stir in sugar, nuts, and coconut.

In saucepan combine ¾ cup water and pectin. Bring to boiling; boil 1 minute, stirring constantly. Stir into fruit mixture; continue cooking and stirring 3 minutes. Ladle into jelly glasses; seal. Let stand till set, about 24 hours. For use within 2 to 3 weeks, store in refrigerator. Makes 6 cups.

Cranberry–Pear Marmalade

Remove peel from 1 lemon; snip peel into fine shreds about 1 inch long. Measure ¼ cup snipped peel and 2 tablespoons lemon juice into large kettle. Add one 14-ounce jar cranberry-orange relish; 3 fresh pears, peeled, cored, and ground; and 2 cups sugar. Bring to full, rolling boil over high heat. Boil hard for 5 minutes; stir occasionally. Pour into hot, clean jars. Seal. Chill. Makes 3⅓ cups.

SUGAR PEA—An alternate name for edible podded peas or Chinese pea pods. (See also *Chinese Pea Pods*.)

SUGAR PLUM—A name applied to especially sweet, small candies and confections. They are also called bonbons.

SUKIYAKI (*sōō′ kē yä′ kē, sōōk′ ē-, skē yä′ ke*)—A Japanese stew of thinly sliced meat, usually beef, and vegetables, simmered in a broth, and seasoned with soy sauce (shoyu) and a bit of sugar. Variations are sometimes prepared with chicken, pork, duck, game, oysters, or clams. This dish is traditionally cooked at the table and served directly from the pan.

The word, sukiyaki, is derived from the Japanese words *suki*, meaning plow, and *yaki*, meaning roasted. This is because, in early times, hunters and farmers cooked meat out in the field on an iron plate, sometimes a plowshare, over an open fire. Today, however, the familiar sukiyaki dish is more of a stew than a roast.

Sukiyaki is an authentic Japanese dish belonging to the class of foods called *nabemono*, which are combinations of meat and vegetables cooked in a saucepan. Sukiyaki is ready to eat when the vegetables are heated through—they should still be slightly crisp.

To prepare a dinner party featuring sukiyaki in the Japanese fashion, arrange the ingredients—meat strips; onions or leeks; bean curd (tofu), if used; mushrooms; and other vegetables—attractively on a large plate. Have containers of broth, soy sauce (shoyu), sugar, and other ingredients premeasured and ready to use.

Set up a low table for dining and seat the guests on pillows on the floor around the table. Then quickly cook the thin strips of meat in an electric skillet or in a skillet over an electric hot plate set on the table. Then add the vegetables. Your guests will enjoy watching as you cook the main dish. Just a hint: Be familiar with how the dish goes together in advance. A trial run before the family is advisable prior to fixing sukiyaki for guests. To accompany this oriental dish, serve steamed rice, the Japanese wine, *sake*, or tea, and dessert.

Sukiyaki

      2 tablespoons salad oil
      1 pound beef tenderloin, sliced paper-thin across the grain
      2 tablespoons sugar
          •   •   •
    ½ cup beef stock *or* canned condensed beef broth
    ⅓ cup soy sauce
          •   •   •
      2 cups 2-inch length bias-cut green onion
      1 cup 1-inch bias-cut celery slices
      1 cup thinly sliced fresh mushrooms
      1 5-ounce can water chestnuts, drained and thinly sliced
      1 5-ounce can bamboo shoots, drained
      5 cups small fresh spinach leaves
      1 16-ounce can bean sprouts, drained
    12 to 16 ounces bean curd, cubed* (optional)
          •   •   •
        Steamed rice
        Soy sauce

Preheat large skillet or electric skillet; add oil. Add beef and cook quickly, turning it over and over, just till browned, about 1 or 2 minutes. Sprinkle meat with sugar. Combine beef stock and soy sauce; pour over meat in skillet. Push the meat to one side of the skillet. Let the soy sauce mixture bubble.

Keeping in separate groups, add onion and celery. Continue cooking and toss-stirring *each group* over high heat about 1 minute; push to one side. Again keeping in separate groups, add mushrooms, chestnuts, bamboo shoots, spinach, bean sprouts, and bean curd. Cook each food just till heated through, lifting vegetables gently to stir. Let guests help themselves to some of everything. Serve with rice. Pass soy sauce. Makes 4 servings.

*Bean curd (tofu) can be purchased at Japanese food shops or obtained from mail-order houses that specialize in oriental foods.

SUMATRA TEA—A fermented tea grown on the island of Sumatra in Indonesia.

Popular varieties of summer squash include zucchini, the cylindrical, lacy green and yellow squash; pattypan, the disk-shaped squash with scalloped edge; and yellow crookneck.

SUMMER SQUASH — Any squash variety that is picked prior to maturation. Both rind and skin of summer squash are soft enough to eat. Known as vegetable marrows in Europe, the following squash are the most commonly used varieties in this general class: chayote, crookneck, straightneck, pattypan, and zucchini.

Because summer squash is primarily composed of water, it is low in calories (15 calories per half cup of cooked squash). Moderate amounts of vitamin C and fair levels of vitamin A and the B vitamin, niacin, are present.

The name summer squash indicates the peak availability—in the summer months. Select squash that is firm, shiny-skinned, and heavy for its size. It should have a characteristic varietal shape.

The storage of summer squash is very limited due to its immaturity. Refrigerate it in the vegetable crisper.

Since summer squash is eaten in its entirety, wash the squash thoroughly before cooking, but do not peel. Remove stem and blossom ends. Cook briefly by boiling, frying, or baking until the pulp is crisp-tender. To serve, simply season with salt and pepper and add a bit of butter. Or, devise dressed-up variations using brown sugar, honey, cheese, bouillon, basil, bay leaf, mace, marjoram, mustard, or rosemary. You can use summer squash by itself, with a stuffing mixture, or with a combination of other vegetables. Some varieties are also delicious when marinated in dressing and served as a salad. (See also *Squash*.)

Company Squash Bake

Cut 1 pound yellow summer squash and 1 medium onion into ¼-inch slices. Cook in boiling, salted water till vegetables are tender. Drain well. In saucepan melt 2 tablespoons butter. Blend in 3 tablespoons all-purpose flour. Add 1 cup milk all at once. Cook, stirring constantly, till thickened and bubbly. Add 4 ounces sharp process American cheese, shredded (1 cup), and one 3-ounce can sliced mushrooms, drained. Stir till cheese melts.

Arrange *half* the squash and onion in a 1½-quart casserole. Cover with *half* the sauce mixture. Repeat layers. Toss together ½ cup soft bread crumbs, ¼ cup chopped pecans, and 1 tablespoon melted butter. Sprinkle atop casserole. Bake, uncovered, at 350° till hot, about 30 minutes. Makes 6 to 8 servings.

Zucchini Vinaigrette

  ¼ cup dry sauterne
  1 envelope Italian salad dressing
        mix
          •   •   •
  ½ cup salad *or* olive oil
  ¼ cup white wine vinegar
  3 to 4 tablespoons finely sliced
        green onion
  3 tablespoons drained
        pickle relish
  2 tablespoons finely snipped
        parsley
  2 tablespoons finely chopped
        green pepper
          •   •   •
  5 or 6 medium zucchini
  3 or 4 medium tomatoes, chilled
        and sliced

For dressing, combine wine and salad dressing mix in a screw-top jar; cover and shake. Add salad oil and next 5 ingredients.

Slice each zucchini in 6 lengthwise strips. Cook in boiling, salted water just till the squash is tender, about 3 to 5 minutes. Drain; arrange in a shallow dish. Shake the dressing and pour over zucchini. Cover and refrigerate several hours or overnight, spooning dressing over occasionally. To serve, drain zucchini and arrange on lettuce-lined platter with tomatoes. Makes 8 or 9 servings.

SUNDAE—A serving of ice cream topped with a sauce. The sauces come in all flavors and varieties as do the ice creams. Gild the lily if you like with toppings of nuts, whipped cream, and/or candied fruit. (See also *Ice Cream Sundae.*)

Tropical Sundaes

     Raspberry, pineapple, and
        lime sherbet
          •   •   •
  1 7-ounce jar marshmallow creme
  3 tablespoons light rum
  ¼ cup flaked coconut

Use wide, stemmed sherbet glasses. For each serving, place a large scoop of raspberry sherbet in each glass. Using a melon baller, add scoops of pineapple and lime sherbets. Top with another large scoop of raspberry sherbet. Freeze till serving time.

In a saucepan stir marshmallow creme over low heat till softened. Blend in rum and coconut. Cool. Stir before serving. Drizzle sauce over sherbet. Makes about 1¼ cups sauce.

Golden Sundaes

In a saucepan combine ½ cup sugar, 2 tablespoons cornstarch, and ⅛ teaspoon ground cinnamon. Gradually blend in 2 cups apricot nectar. Add 1 teaspoon grated orange peel. Cook and stir till mixture thickens and bubbles. Remove from heat. Stir in 4 or 5 medium apricots, cut into chunks (1 cup). Chill thoroughly. To serve, scoop vanilla ice cream into dishes. Top with chilled sauce. Makes 8 servings.

Sundae Special

In a heavy saucepan combine one 12-ounce package semisweet chocolate pieces (2 cups), 1 cup miniature marshmallows, and ¼ cup light corn syrup. Cook and stir till chocolate and marshmallows are melted. Remove from heat. Gradually stir in one 7-ounce bottle lemon-lime carbonated beverage (about 1 cup). Add 1 teaspoon vanilla. To serve, scoop vanilla or peppermint ice cream into dishes. Top with sauce. Makes 2⅓ cups.

Tropical Sundaes are made with several flavors of sherbet topped with a coconut- and rum-flavored marshmallow sauce.

SUNFISH—A group of fish native to North America and found living in both salt and fresh water. The ocean sunfish is a large, round, and somewhat flat fish and can weigh several hundred pounds. It is usually found in the warm waters off the California coast but is rarely eaten.

Of more importance as a food is the freshwater sunfish. The three most familiar to fish lovers—bluegill, pumpkinseed, and crappie—are smaller than the ocean sunfish, have a flattened body, and usually are brightly colored. They live in ponds, quiet streams, and lakes. Some kinds of sunfish are desirable as game fish, not only because of their pleasing flavor, but because of the fight they give to the sports fisherman.

Freshwater sunfish average seven to eight inches long and usually weigh about eight ounces. They are especially delicious when they are either broiled or panfried. (See also *Fish.*)

SUNFLOWER SEED—The edible seed of certain varieties of the sunflower plant, made popular by health food lovers. However, they are by no means a new food. The Incas ate them hundreds of years ago during certain religious ceremonies. This was probably because the sunflower plant from which the seeds came was also worshiped as the sun.

The Spanish introduced the sunflower plant to Europe, where the seeds of certain types were used not only as a food, but to produce a pale yellow, mildly flavored oil. Today, the seeds are dried, roasted, salted, and eaten as a snack.

SUPPER—A light meal that is served in the evening, especially when the main meal is served at noon. It can also be a late evening meal, when dinner is served earlier in the evening. The late-evening supper can be as elaborate as an entrée of Lobster Newburg, or as simple as scrambled eggs and sausages.

SUPRÊME SAUCE—A white sauce based on Velouté Sauce, which is made with chicken stock. Cream is added before serving for extra richness. This sauce is used most often on poultry and meat.

SURF CLAM—A type of clam found along the Atlantic coast. Although surf clams are the most abundant, they are not as highly prized as the soft-shell or hard clams. (See also *Clam.*)

SURINAM CHERRY *(soor' uh näm')*—A red, cherrylike fruit of a Brazilian shrub now grown in Florida and California. The cherries can be eaten raw, although they are usually made into jam or jelly.

SWEDE TURNIP—An alternate name for rutabaga. Sometimes, this name is shortened to Swede. (See also *Rutabaga.*)

SWEDISH COOKERY—The cuisine of a country which is well-known for its smörgasbord, fresh and pickled fish, meats, sauced vegetables, home-baked breads, and a variety of delicate and hearty pastries. Though Swedish food is often less elaborate than that of many other European countries, it is always attractively arranged and garnished.

Sweden is an agricultural country with an abundance of vegetables, cereal grains, fruits, and berries. Its long seacoast makes it natural that fish and shellfish are plentifully used in recipe preparation. Before the modern kingdom of Sweden was established with its present boundaries, all of the other Scandinavian countries were, at sometime, joined with Sweden under common rule. This accounts for the family resemblance in the cookery of all the Scandinavian countries. Yet Swedish cooks have traditionally made use of their local foods to give their cooking a distinctive character. The Swedish herring salad (*Sillsallad*), for example, with apples and beets, is dressed with cream reddened with beet juice, making it distinguishably Swedish.

The Swedish smörgasbord (bread and butter table) is, undoubtedly, the best known presentation of Swedish food. It has been adopted and adapted in many other countries. For the traditional smörgasbord, definite rules of etiquette demand enjoyment of the food in courses, with a fresh plate for each: herring, other cold fish dishes and/or cold egg dishes, followed by cold meats and salads, hot foods, and finally cheese.

Though fresh meats and fish are popular in Sweden, salt-cured, smoked, and pickled products are also enjoyed. Salted and dilled salmon (*Gravad Lax*) cut in slices is a treat. Other dishes include boiled, pickled goose with horseradish cream sauce, herring pudding (*Sillpudding*) made with salt herring, and yellow pea soup with salt pork.

But fresh meats have their fair share of the cuisine, too, and often are served with dill sauce or potato dumplings. Freshly ground beef, veal, and pork are made into meatballs (*Köttbullar*) which are fried in butter and served with a cream gravy. Boiled lamb is delicious with dill sauce, and veal cutlets are stuffed with a parsley butter mixture.

Vegetables to accompany the meats are usually sauced, often mashed. Traditionally, Swedish brown beans go with fried pork or meatballs, red cabbage with goose or ham, and mashed turnips with boiled sausage. Salads, such as dilled cucumber slices, are served as a relish, rather than on lettuce leaves.

As bakers, Swedish cooks shine. Sturdy loaves of dark caraway rye and big, crisp, flat wheels of *Knäckebrod* vie with sweet, leavened *Limpa*, a cakelike rye bread flavored with caraway or orange peel. White flour produces breads, cakes, and coffee cakes and rolls, rich with fillings of nuts, fruits, and spices. Delicate pancakes (*Plättar*) frequently are baked in a special pan and served with lingonberries.

There are many kinds of cookies and desserts, including butter-rich *Spritsar*, crullerlike *Klenäter*, gingery *Pepparkakor*, and tiny pastry tarts with buttery almond filling, to name only a few. There are also rosettes, fried in deep fat and sprinkled with sugar; apple cake served with vanilla sauce; clabbered milk sprinkled with sugar and spices; rice porridge; fruit soups; and filled wafers. (See also *Scandinavian Cookery*.)

Swedish Ginger Cookies

A favorite holiday treat—

>   1 cup butter
> 1½ cups sugar
>   1 egg
> 1½ tablespoons grated orange peel
>   2 tablespoons dark corn syrup
> 3¼ cups sifted all-purpose flour
>   2 teaspoons baking soda
>   2 teaspoons ground cinnamon
>   1 teaspoon ground ginger
>   ½ teaspoon ground cloves
>   Toasted blanched almonds

Cream butter and sugar. Add egg; beat till fluffy. Add peel, corn syrup, and 1 tablespoon water; mix. Sift together dry ingredients. Stir into creamed mixture; chill. On lightly floured surface, roll dough ⅛ inch thick. Sprinkle dough with sugar. Press in lightly with rolling pin. Cut with floured, scalloped or diamond cutter. Place 1 inch apart on *ungreased* cookie sheet. Top each with an almond. Bake at 375° for 8 to 10 minutes. Cool slightly before removing from pan. Makes about 8 dozen.

SWEET—1. Food that contains a high proportion of sugar, such as candies and desserts. **2.** A taste sensation. **3.** A nickname for sweet potatoes (sweets).

SWEET BASIL—An alternate name for the herb, basil. (See also *Basil.*)

SWEETBREAD—The thymus gland from the neck or throat of young animals—veal, calf, or lamb. (This gland appears as the animal matures.) Sweetbreads from veal and calves are usually marketed. Although not widely available, some sweetbreads also come from the pancreas.

Sweetbreads are a source of protein, some minerals, the B vitamins thiamine, riboflavin, and niacin, vitamin A, and relative large amounts of vitamin C. A half pair of average-sized sweetbreads contains about 184 calories.

Sweetbreads are considered to be a delicacy. They are very perishable and must be cooked or frozen immediately after purchase. If you are not planning to use them right away, it's advisable to precook and then refrigerate them.

After the sweetbreads are washed and the membranes removed, popular methods of preparation include braising, broiling, and frying. They may also be used in creamed mixtures. Prepared these ways, the sweetbreads should be precooked in salted water to which lemon juice or vinegar is added to keep them white and firm. (See also *Variety Meat.*)

Sweetbread Bake

Simmer 1 pound sweetbreads in a mixture of 1 quart water, 1 tablespoon lemon juice, and 1 teaspoon salt for 20 minutes. Cut into 6 serving-sized pieces. Dip into a mixture of 1 slightly beaten egg and 1 tablespoon water, then into ½ cup fine dry bread crumbs. Using 6 slices bacon, wrap each piece in bacon and fasten with wooden pick. Bake in shallow pan at 400° for 35 minutes. Serves 4 to 6.

SWEET CHOCOLATE—A chocolate product made from unsweetened chocolate with the addition of sugar and extra cocoa

A sauce made with sweet chocolate is streaked through Hot Fudge Sundae Cake, reminiscent of the familiar ice cream treat. The chocolate glaze makes it a double chocolate winner.

butter. You'll find sweet chocolate available in sectioned bars just right for use in cooking or eating. It is also called sweet cooking chocolate. (See also *Chocolate*.)

Hot Fudge Sundae Cake

```
  3 cups sifted all-purpose flour
  3 teaspoons baking powder
  1 teaspoon salt
½ cup bu ter or margarine
½ cup sh rtening
1½ cups sugar
  4 eggs
  1 cup mi k
  1 teaspoon vanilla
  1 4-ounce bar sweet cooking
       chocolate
  2 tablespoons water
  2 tablespoons milk
            •  •  •
  1 1-ounce square unsweetened
       chocolate
  2 tablespoons butter or margarine
  2 tablespoons milk
  1 cup sifted confectioners' sugar
¼ teaspoon vanilla
⅛ teaspoon salt
```

Sift together flour, baking powder, and 1 teaspoon salt. Cream ½ cup butter and shortening together. Gradually add sugar, creaming till light and fluffy. Add eggs, one at a time, beating 1 minute after each addition. Combine 1 cup milk and 1 teaspoon vanilla. Add alternately with dry ingredients to creamed mixture. Blend well after each addition.

For sauce, melt sweet chocolate with 2 tablespoons water over hot water. Remove from heat and blend in the 2 tablespoons milk.

Turn one-fourth of the batter into a greased 10-inch tube pan. Drizzle with some of the sauce, alternating layers of batter and sauce to make three layers of sauce with batter on top. Bake at 350° till done, 70 to 80 minutes. Cool in pan. Remove from pan.

Make chocolate glaze by heating unsweetened chocolate, 2 tablespoons butter, and 2 tablespoons milk over hot water. Stir till chocolate is melted. Remove from heat. Add confectioners' sugar, ¼ teaspoon vanilla, and ⅛ teaspoon salt. Beat till smooth. Drizzle over top and sides of cake.

Chocolate Éclair Cake

Use sweet chocolate in the icing—

```
  4 1-ounce squares unsweetened
       chocolate, melted
½ cup boiling water
1¾ cups sugar
2¼ cups sifted cake flour
  3 teaspoons baking powder
½ cup salad oil
  7 egg yolks
¾ cup cold water
  1 teaspoon vanilla
  7 egg whites
½ teaspoon cream of tartar
     Custard Filling
     Chocolate Icing
     Confectioners' Sugar Icing
```

Combine chocolate, boiling water, and ¼ *cup* sugar; cool. Sift together flour, remaining sugar, baking powder, and 1 teaspoon salt into bowl. Make well in center of dry ingredients. Add, in order, next 4 ingredients. Beat smooth. Stir in chocolate mixture. In large mixer bowl combine egg whites and cream of tartar; beat till stiff peaks form. Pour chocolate mixture in thin stream over entire surface of whites; fold in gently. Bake in ungreased 10-inch tube pan at 325° for 65 minutes. Invert pan to cool; remove from pan.

Prepare Custard Filling. Using wooden picks for guides, split cake into 3 layers. Fill between layers with Custard Filling. Frost with Chocolate Icing. Immediately pipe Confectioners' Sugar Icing around top; draw knife through icing at regular intervals to give web effect. Chill. Serves 12 to 16.

Custard Filling: In saucepan combine ¼ cup sugar and ¼ cup cornstarch. Stir in 3 cups milk; stir in 2 beaten eggs. Cook and stir till thickened and bubbly; add 2 teaspoons vanilla. Cover surface with waxed paper; cool.

Chocolate Icing: In saucepan melt together one 4-ounce package sweet cooking chocolate and 3 tablespoons butter over low heat. Remove from heat; stir in 1½ cups sifted confectioners' sugar and enough hot water (3 to 4 tablespoons) to make of pouring consistency.

Confectioners' Sugar Icing: Add enough light cream to 1 cup sifted confectioners' sugar to make of spreading consistency. Add dash salt and ½ teaspoon vanilla.

SWEET CICELY—An anise-flavored herb, belonging to the parsley family, with large, feathery, pale green leaves. These are excellent for imparting a delicate flavor to salads and sauces.

SWEETENED CONDENSED MILK—A concentrated milk made from fresh, whole milk to which sugar is added and part of the water is removed under vacuum. This milk, sold in airtight cans, contains about 28 percent milk solids and 8.3 percent milk fat. The consistency of sweetened condensed milk is smooth and thick, and the milk is cream-colored and sticky.

Although sweetened condensed milk supplies the same kind of nutrients as whole milk, they are present in a higher proportion, cup for cup. Since sugar is added to make sweetened condensed milk, the carbohydrate content is also higher than in whole milk. One cup of sweetened condensed milk has 982 calories while one cup of fluid whole milk has about 160 calories.

Nowadays the principal use of condensed milk is for specially-formulated recipes, especially desserts, sauces, ice cream, and candies. It is an entirely different product than evaporated milk and the two cannot be interchanged in recipes.

Store the unopened can on the shelf. Once opened, the can should be refrigerated. (See also *Milk.*)

Peppermint Ice Cream

½ of one 14-ounce can *sweetened condensed* milk (⅔ cup)
½ cup water
½ teaspoon peppermint extract
3 drops red food coloring
. . .
1 cup whipping cream

Combine the milk, water, extract, and food coloring. Whip cream till thick and custardlike; fold into peppermint mixture. Pour mixture into a 3-cup refrigerator tray. Freeze till partially frozen. Break mixture into chunks into a chilled mixer bowl. Beat till smooth. Return immediately to cold refrigerator tray. Freeze till firm. Makes 3 cups.

Chocolate Revel Bars

1 cup butter or margarine
2 cups brown sugar
2 eggs
2 teaspoons vanilla
2½ cups sifted all-purpose flour
1 teaspoon baking soda
1 teaspoon salt
3 cups quick-cooking rolled oats
. . .
1 14-ounce can *sweetened condensed* milk
1 12-ounce package semisweet chocolate pieces (2 cups)
2 tablespoons butter or margarine
½ teaspoon salt
1 cup chopped walnuts
2 teaspoons vanilla

In large bowl cream 1 cup butter and brown sugar. Beat in eggs and 2 teaspoons vanilla. Sift together flour, baking soda, and 1 teaspoon salt; stir in oats. Stir dry ingredients into creamed mixture till blended; set aside. In heavy saucepan heat together sweetened condensed milk, chocolate, 2 tablespoons butter, and ½ teaspoon salt over low heat, stirring till smooth. Stir in chopped nuts and 2 teaspoons vanilla. Pat ⅔ of oat mixture in bottom of 15½x10½x1-inch baking pan. Spread chocolate mixture over dough. Dot with remaining oat mixture. Bake at 350° for 25 to 30 minutes; cool. Cut in 2x1-inch bars. Makes 75 bars.

English Toffee Ice Cream

4 1⅛-ounce chocolate coated English toffee bars
1 14-ounce can *sweetened condensed* milk
½ cup strong coffee, cooled
2 cups whipping cream
1½ teaspoons vanilla

Crush toffee bars by placing them between two pieces of waxed paper and crushing with rolling pin; set aside. Combine sweetened condensed milk, coffee, whipping cream, and vanilla. Chill thoroughly. Whip the mixture to custardlike consistency. Fold in the crushed toffee bars. Spoon into three 3-cup refrigerator trays. Freeze firm. Makes 8 cups.

Chocolate Fondue

Choose coffee, mint, brandy, or orange liqueur as a flavor partner with the chocolate—

8 1-ounce squares semisweet
    chocolate
1 14-ounce can *sweetened condensed*
    milk (1⅓ cups)
⅓ cup milk
2 tablespoons instant coffee powder
    or 4 ounces cream-filled mint
    patties *or* ¼ cup brandy *or* ⅓
    cup orange-flavored liqueur

• • •

Cookies, angel cake squares,
    banana or pineapple chunks

In saucepan melt chocolate; stir in sweetened condensed milk and regular milk till well blended. Heat through. Stir in coffee powder, mint patties, brandy, *or* orange liqueur. Pour into fondue pot. Place over fondue burner. (If desired, thin fondue with more milk; fondue will thicken as it stands.) Use as dip for cookies, angel cake, banana chunks, pineapple chunks, or other fruits. Makes 2½ cups sauce.

Choco-Mallow Ice Cream

Tastes like the popular rocky road ice cream—

½ of one 14-ounce can *sweetened*
    condensed milk (⅔ cup)
1 1-ounce square unsweetened
    chocolate
½ cup water
½ teaspoon vanilla
1 cup whipping cream
1 cup tiny marshmallows
½ cup chopped walnuts

In top of double boiler combine milk and chocolate; place over *hot, not boiling*, water. Cook, stirring often, till thick, about 10 minutes. Slowly add water and vanilla; mix well. Chill. Whip cream till thick and custardlike; fold into chocolate mixture. Pour into a 3-cup refrigerator tray; freeze till firm. Break mixture into chunks into a chilled bowl. Beat till smooth. Fold in marshmallows and nuts. Quickly return mixture to cold tray; freeze till firm. Makes about 1½ pints.

Pineapple Freeze

1 cup dairy sour cream
1 14-ounce can *sweetened condensed*
    milk (1⅓ cups)
2 cups milk
1 tablespoon lemon juice
1 8¾-ounce can crushed
    pineapple, drained

Combine dairy sour cream and *sweetened condensed* milk. Stir in milk and lemon juice. Freeze mixture in 1-quart refrigerator tray till partially frozen. Stir in drained pineapple; freeze till firm. Makes 1 quart.

Peanut Coco-Roons

1⅓ cups flaked coconut
½ cup *sweetened condensed* milk
    Dash salt
1 teaspoon vanilla
1 1-ounce square unsweetened
    chocolate, melted
¾ cup coarsely chopped peanuts

Combine flaked coconut, *sweetened condensed* milk, salt, vanilla, melted chocolate, and chopped peanuts. Drop from teaspoon onto a greased baking sheet, 1 inch apart. Bake at 350° for 8 to 10 minutes. Remove from baking sheet at once. Makes about 2 dozen.

SWEET FENNEL *(fen' uhl)*—One of the cultivated varieties of a wild herb. This herb is used not only as a flavoring ingredient but also used as a vegetable and garnish. Its fernlike leaves resemble dill and its stalks, as they form a fat bulb, resemble celery. Sweet fennel is found in the market among the salad greens. It may be labeled Florence fennel or finnocchio. (See also *Fennel*.)

SWEET MARJORAM—A perennial herb with aromatic, gray-green leaves. Its flavor is pleasantly spicy and sweet but not so pungent as that of oregano, marjoram's close relative. This herb is used to flavor vegetables, meats, and stews. It is one of the basic ingredients in poultry seasoning mixtures. (See also *Marjoram*.)

SWEET POTATO—An enlarged, tuberlike root of a tropical vine that is eaten as a vegetable. It is not a member of the common white potato family but is related to the morning glory.

Sweet potatoes are native to tropical America where they were being cultivated and eaten by natives before the Spanish first explored South America.

The sweet flavor of this tuber was so well-liked by the Spanish that samples were taken back to Europe. Later, Europeans introduced them to the Far East and to North America. Sweet potatoes were being grown in Virginia by 1648 and in the northeast by 1764.

In various nations, sweet potatoes have become commercially important for their food value as well as for the by-products that can be made from them. South Americans incorporate sweet potatoes into their daily diets. After rice, sweet potatoes are the biggest food crop grown in Japan where they are used to make alcohol, starch, and animal feed. In the United States, they are one of the top ten vegetables produced.

How sweet potatoes are produced: Because the plants are indigenous to tropical climates, in the United States they are grown primarily in southern regions. Some varieties have been adapted to cooler climates, thus making it possible for California and states along the Atlantic Coast as far north as New Jersey to become substantial producers. Sprouts that grow out of the roots are used for propagation rather than seeds.

When harvesting has been completed, sweet potatoes must be cured prior to marketing. They are first stored under conditions of high temperature and humidity for 7 to 10 days, after which the sweet potatoes are held under temperature conditions of 50° to 55° until they are marketed. This procedure reduces the onset of deterioration and decay.

Nutritional value: Sweet potatoes are higher in sugar content than white potatoes and contain substantially more calories. From small to large size, they yield about 140 to 250 calories.

Sweet potatoes also are an excellent source of vitamins and minerals. They contain high quantities of vitamin A, good amounts of vitamin C, fair amounts of the B vitamin, thiamine, as well as smaller quantities of other nutrients.

Types of sweet potatoes: Although there are many varieties of sweet potatoes that range in skin color from white to brown or purple and in flesh color from yellow to deep orange, there are two main types produced in the United States.

The first type is identified by a light yellow to pale orange skin and light yellow flesh. When cooked, the interior has a dry, mealy texture.

Orange, pale rose, or copper skin and bright to red orange flesh identifies the second type, a sweeter, denser, and more moist sweet potato most popular in the South. They are often referred to as yams, although this is technically incorrect.

How to select: The largest number of fresh sweet potatoes is available in the fall and early winter, although in some localities they are found year-round. Select sweet potatoes with good shape;

A wreath of sliced Canadian bacon hides a savory grape and mashed sweet potato combo. Sweet Potato Fantasia is a meal-in-one dish.

smooth, bright, uniform skin color; and firm texture. Avoid those with decay, wet spots, or soft, dry, and shriveled areas.

In addition to fresh sweet potatoes, modern processing techniques have made available canned, frozen, and dehydrated forms. These processed sweet potatoes may be purchased cut in assorted sizes, or packed plain or in a syrup, depending on personal preference.

How to store: Sweet potatoes are much more perishable than white potatoes. They can be stored in a cool, dry place of about 55° for a short time only. Since sweet potatoes are susceptible to decay under moist conditions, they should not be stored in the refrigerator.

How to prepare and use: Whether they are to be baked, boiled, or fried, sweet potatoes should first be scrubbed and any woody portions removed.

Although more nutritive value is retained if sweet potatoes are cooked in the skins, the recipe itself finally determines whether the skins should be peeled off prior to cooking. Bake whole, unpeeled sweet potatoes at 375° for 40 to 45 minutes; or boil them, covered, in salted water for 30 to 40 minutes. In general, dry varieties require more cooking time than the moist ones. Fried sweet potatoes are peeled, cut in desired shapes, and either panfried or deep-fat fried.

French-Fried Sweet Potatoes

Wash and peel 3 medium sweet potatoes. Slice uncooked potatoes in ½- to ¾-inch-thick sticks; soak in ice water for 1 to 2 hours. Dry thoroughly between paper toweling. Fry in deep, hot fat (365°) till browned, 3 to 5 minutes; drain. Salt to taste. Makes about 4 cups.

As a vegetable side dish, sweet potatoes may be mashed with butter or combined with other vegetables, fruits, or seasonings including allspice, cardamom, cinnamon, cloves, ginger, nutmeg, and poppy seed. They make a popular Thanksgiving and Christmas combo served with turkey

or ham. Southerners also enjoy sweet potatoes in a variety of baked goods such as breads, pies, cookies, and cakes.

Mashed Sweet Potatoes

Peel hot, cooked sweet potatoes; mash. Beat till fluffy, gradually adding hot milk as needed. Beat in salt, pepper, and butter to taste.

Candied Sweet Potatoes

      6 medium sweet potatoes, cooked
          and peeled
   ¾ cup brown sugar
   1 teaspoon salt
   ¼ cup butter or margarine
   ½ cup miniature marshmallows

Cut sweet potatoes in ½-inch slices. Ending with sugar and butter, layer potatoes in buttered 1½-quart casserole with brown sugar, salt, and butter. Bake, uncovered, at 375° till glazed, about 30 minutes. Add marshmallows last 5 minutes; brown lightly. Makes 6 servings.

California Potato Bake

      4 medium sweet potatoes*
   ½ cup brown sugar
   1 tablespoon cornstarch
   ¼ teaspoon salt
   1 cup orange juice
   ¼ cup seedless raisins
   ¼ cup butter or margarine
   3 tablespoons dry sherry
   2 tablespoons chopped walnuts
   ½ teaspoon shredded orange peel

Cook potatoes in boiling, salted water till tender. Drain; peel and halve lengthwise.* Arrange the potatoes in shallow baking dish or pan. Sprinkle lightly with salt.

In a saucepan mix brown sugar, cornstarch, and salt. Blend in orange juice; add raisins. Cook and stir over high heat till mixture comes to boiling. Add the remaining ingredients; pour over potatoes. Bake, uncovered, at 350° till potatoes are well-glazed, about 20 minutes. Makes 4 servings.

*Or use one 18-ounce can sweet potatoes.

Stuffed Sweet Potatoes

Select 6 medium sweet potatoes. Scrub. Bake at 425° till done, about 40 minutes. (*Or* if sweet potatoes share oven with other foods, bake at 350° to 375° about 1 hour.) Cut slice from top of each. Scoop out inside, being careful not to break shell. Mash the potatoes.

To mashed sweet potatoes, add ¼ cup softened butter or margarine, 1 tablespoon brown sugar, 1 teaspoon salt, dash pepper, and enough hot milk to moisten. Beat until fluffy. Fold in ⅓ cup miniature marshmallows and ¼ cup chopped walnuts.

Pile mixture lightly into the potato shells. Top with additional ⅓ cup miniature marshmallows. Bake in 350° oven till heated through and browned, about 15 to 20 minutes.

Sweet Potato-Frank Skillet

   ¼ cup butter or margarine
   2 tablespoons prepared mustard
   ¾ cup dark corn syrup
   ½ teaspoon salt
   1 pound frankfurters
   4 or 5 medium sweet potatoes, cooked, peeled, and quartered *or* one 18-ounce can sweet potatoes, drained
   1 medium orange, peeled and coarsely chopped

In large skillet melt butter; blend in mustard, corn syrup, and salt. Score frankfurters at 1-inch intervals; add frankfurters, sweet potatoes, and orange to skillet. Cover and simmer slowly for 15 minutes, basting occasionally with the glaze. Makes 4 or 5 servings.

Maple-Flavored Sweets

   6 medium sweet potatoes
   ½ cup maple-flavored syrup
   1 tablespoon butter or margarine
   ½ cup apple cider *or* apple juice

Boil potatoes in jackets till nearly tender; peel and slice into a 10x6x1¾-inch baking dish. Heat remaining ingredients and 1 teaspoon salt to boiling; pour over potatoes and bake at 350° for about 45 minutes, basting occasionally. Makes 6 to 8 servings.

Apricot-Sweet Potatoes

   1 18-ounce can sweet potatoes, sliced
   1¼ cups brown sugar
   1½ tablespoons cornstarch
   1 teaspoon grated orange peel
   ¼ teaspoon salt
   ⅛ teaspoon ground cinnamon
   1 17-ounce can apricot halves
   2 tablespoons butter or margarine
   ½ cup pecan halves

Arrange potatoes in a lightly greased 10x6x1¾-inch baking dish. Combine next 5 ingredients. Drain apricots, reserving 1 cup syrup; add syrup to sugar mixture. Cook and stir over medium heat; simmer 3 minutes. Add apricots, butter, and pecans. Bring to boiling; boil 2 minutes. Pour over potatoes. Bake, uncovered, at 375° for 25 minutes. Makes 6 servings.

Sweet Potato Fantasia

   2 3½-ounce packages instant sweet potatoes
   1 slightly beaten egg
   2 tablespoons brown sugar
   ½ cup seedless green grapes
   ¼ cup broken pecans
   ½ pound Canadian-style bacon, sliced

Prepare potatoes according to package directions; cool. Stir in egg, brown sugar, and ¼ teaspoon salt. Fold in grapes and pecans. Pile into a 1-quart casserole. Bake, uncovered, at 350° for 25 minutes. Top with bacon slices. Return to oven; bake 15 minutes more. Garnish with additional grapes, if desired. Serves 4 to 6.

Toasted Croquettes

Mix 2 cups mashed, cooked sweet potatoes; 1 tablespoon brown sugar; 2 tablespoons butter, melted; 1 teaspoon salt; and dash pepper. Shape mixture into 12 balls around 12 marshmallows. Roll in additional melted butter, then in ½ cup fine dry bread crumbs.

Fry in a skillet with 3 tablespoons melted butter till brown. *Or* bake in a shallow baking pan at 350° for 15 minutes. Makes 12.

Fruit-Candied Sweet Potatoes bake in pineapple-orange juice concentrate sweetened with brown sugar. Pecans garnish the top.

Fruit-Candied Sweet Potatoes

     1 16-ounce can sweet potatoes *or* 6
          cooked medium sweet potatoes
    ½ cup brown sugar
     2 tablespoons butter or margarine
    ½ 6-ounce can frozen pineapple-
          orange juice concentrate,
          thawed (⅓ cup)
    ¼ cup coarsely chopped pecans

Halve potatoes lengthwise; arrange in a greased 1-quart casserole. Sprinkle with brown sugar; dot with butter. Spoon juice concentrate over all. Cover; bake at 325° for 45 minutes. Garnish with nuts. Makes 4 to 6 servings.

Sweet Potato Boats

Cook 3 large sweet potatoes in boiling, salted water just till tender. Remove skins. Cut in half lengthwise. Spoon out centers of sweet potato halves. Combine sweet potato centers and ½ cup cranberry-orange relish; beat till fluffy. Stir in ¼ cup seedless raisins. Spoon the mixture into potato halves.

Combine ⅓ cup brown sugar and ½ teaspoon salt; cut in 3 tablespoons butter. Stir in ¼ cup chopped walnuts. Sprinkle over sweet potatoes. Bake at 350° for 30 minutes. Serves 6.

Sweet Potato Puff

Orange peel adds special flavor to sweet potatoes—

     2 cups hot, mashed, cooked sweet
          potatoes
    ½ cup milk
     2 tablespoons butter or margarine
    ½ teaspoon salt
    ½ teaspoon grated orange peel
          Dash ground allspice
     2 egg yolks
     2 egg whites
          Butter or margarine

Combine potato, milk, butter, salt, orange peel, and allspice in a large mixing bowl. Beat with electric mixer or rotary beater till fluffy. Add egg yolks; beat well. Beat egg whites to stiff peaks; fold in potato mixture. Turn into *ungreased* 1-quart soufflé dish.

Bake the mixture at 350° till heated through, about 55 to 60 minutes. Serve with butter or margarine. Makes 6 servings.

Sweet Potato–Date Bake

Quick to make for holiday meals—

     1 18-ounce can sweet potatoes
    ¼ cup light cream
    ⅛ teaspoon ground cinnamon
    ½ teaspoon salt
    ½ cup snipped pitted dates
     2 tablespoons butter or margarine,
          melted

Heat sweet potatoes; mash while hot. Add cream, cinnamon, salt, dates, and butter. Mix well and turn into a buttered 1-quart casserole. Bake at 350° till light brown, about 20 to 25 minutes. Makes 6 servings.

SWEET ROLL—A variety of rolls made with a sweet dough and filled, garnished, or flavored with fruits, nuts, sugar, and spices. Some sweet rolls are frosted while others are not. This is the category for sticky buns or caramel rolls, Danish rolls, cinnamon buns, and the like. Sweet rolls make perfect midmorning snacks to be enjoyed with a cup of coffee or tea.

Glazed Orange Rolls

    1 package active dry yeast
4½ cups sifted all-purpose flour
    1 cup milk
    3 tablespoons butter or margarine
    ½ cup granulated sugar
    ½ teaspoon salt
    3 eggs

• • •

    6 tablespoons butter or margarine,
       softened
    ½ cup granulated sugar
1½ teaspoons shredded orange peel

• • •

    2 cups sifted confectioners'
       sugar
    3 to 4 tablespoons orange juice

In large mixer bowl combine yeast and 2½ *cups* of the flour. Heat milk, 3 tablespoons butter or margarine, ½ cup granulated sugar, and salt just till warm, stirring occasionally to melt butter. Add to dry mixture in mixing bowl. Add eggs. Beat at low speed with electric mixer for ½ minute, scraping sides of bowl constantly. Beat 3 minutes at high speed. By hand stir in enough of the remaining flour to make a moderately stiff dough.

   Turn out onto a floured surface; knead till smooth and satiny, about 10 minutes. Place in greased bowl, turning to coat surface. Cover; let rise till double, about 2 hours. Divide dough in half. Roll each to a 12x8-inch rectangle. Stir together the 6 tablespoons softened butter, ½ cup granulated sugar, and shredded orange peel. Spread over dough. Roll up each piece of dough, starting with long side. Seal seams. Slice each into 18 rolls. Place, cut side down, in greased 2½-inch muffin pans. (Or use three 9-inch round baking pans.) Let rise till double, about 1½ hours. Bake at 375° till the rolls are done, about 15 minutes.

   Combine confectioners' sugar and enough orange juice to make of glaze consistency. Drizzle over warm rolls. Makes 3 dozen rolls.

Sweet rolls warm from the oven

Like many other yeast breads, Glazed Orange Rolls are not quick to make but they are worth every moment of the preparation.

Caramel-Pecan Rolls

A favorite of all ages—

   3½ to 4 cups sifted all-purpose
        flour
     1 package active dry yeast
     1 cup milk
   ¼ cup granulated sugar
   ¼ cup shortening
     1 teaspoon salt
     2 eggs
     3 tablespoons butter or margarine,
        melted
   ½ cup granulated sugar
     1 teaspoon ground cinnamon

       . . .

   ⅔ cup brown sugar
   ¼ cup butter or margarine
     2 tablespoons light corn syrup
   ½ cup chopped pecans

In large mixer bowl combine *2 cups* of the all-purpose flour and active dry yeast. Heat milk, ¼ cup granulated sugar, shortening, and salt till warm (115-120°), stirring to melt shortening. Add to dry mixture; add eggs. Beat at low speed with electric mixer for ½ minute, scraping sides of bowl constantly. Beat 3 minutes at high speed. By hand, stir in enough remaining flour to make a moderately stiff dough. Knead on lightly floured surface till smooth (8 to 10 minutes). Shape into a ball. Place in greased bowl, turning once to grease surface. Cover; let dough rise till double (45 to 60 minutes). Punch dough down; divide in half. Cover; let dough rest 10 minutes.

Roll each half of the roll dough into a 12x8-inch rectangle. Brush *each* with *half* the melted butter or margarine. Combine ½ cup granulated sugar and cinnamon; sprinkle over dough. Roll up each piece of dough, starting with long side; seal seams. Slice each roll into 12 pieces. In saucepan combine brown sugar, ¼ cup butter or margarine, and corn syrup. Cook and stir just till butter melts and mixture is blended. Distribute brown sugar mixture evenly in two 9x1½-inch round baking pans. Top with chopped pecans. Place rolls, cut side down, in prepared baking pans. Cover; let rise till double (about 30 minutes). Bake sweet rolls at 375° for 18 to 20 minutes. Cool about 30 seconds; invert rolls on rack and remove pans. Makes 24 sweet rolls.

Cinnamon Crisps

   3½ cups sifted all-purpose flour
     1 package active dry yeast
  1¼ cups milk
   ¼ cup granulated sugar
   ¼ cup shortening
     1 teaspoon salt
     1 egg
   ¼ cup butter or margarine, melted
   ½ cup brown sugar
   ½ cup granulated sugar
   ½ teaspoon ground cinnamon
   ¼ cup butter or margarine, melted
     1 cup granulated sugar
   ½ cup chopped pecans
     1 teaspoon ground cinnamon

In large mixer bowl combine *2 cups* of the flour and the yeast. In saucepan heat milk, ¼ cup granulated sugar, shortening, and salt just till warm (115-120°), stirring constantly to melt shortening. Add to dry ingredients in mixer bowl; add egg. Beat at low speed with electric mixer for ½ minute, scraping sides of bowl constantly. Beat 3 minutes at high speed. By hand, stir in enough of the remaining flour to make a moderately soft dough. Shape into a ball. Place dough in a lightly greased bowl, turning once to grease surface. Cover and let rise in a warm place until double (1½ to 2 hours). Punch down; turn out on lightly floured surface. Divide dough in half. Cover; let the dough rest 10 minutes.

Roll out one portion of dough at a time to a 12-inch square. Combine ¼ cup melted butter, brown sugar, ½ cup granulated sugar, and ½ teaspoon ground cinnamon. Spread *half* of mixture over dough. Roll up lengthwise jelly-roll fashion; pinch to seal edges. Cut into 12 rolls. Place on greased baking sheets at least 3 inches apart. Flatten each to 3 inches in diameter. Repeat with remaining dough and sugar mixture. Let rise in warm place (about 30 minutes).

Cover with waxed paper. Roll over tops with rolling pin to flatten to about ⅛-inch thickness. Carefully remove waxed paper. Brush tops of rolls with remaining melted butter. Combine remaining 1 cup granulated sugar, pecans, and 1 teaspoon ground cinnamon. Sprinkle over rolls. Cover with waxed paper and roll flat again. Bake at 400° for 10 to 12 minutes. Remove immediately from baking sheets to cooling racks. Makes 24 rolls.

Peanut Butter–Jelly Twists

2¼ cups sifted all-purpose flour
1 package active dry yeast
½ cup milk
¼ cup sugar
4 tablespoons butter or margarine
1 egg
⅓ cup peanut butter
⅓ cup red jam or preserves

In large mixer bowl combine *1 cup* of the flour and the yeast. Heat milk, sugar, *3 tablespoons* butter, and 1 teaspoon salt till warm (115-120°), stirring to melt butter. Add to dry mixture; add egg. Beat at low speed with mixer for ½ minute, scraping bowl. Beat 3 minutes at high speed. Stir in remaining flour; beat well. Cover; let rest ½ hour. Roll dough to 16x10-inch rectangle. Spread peanut butter over lengthwise half; spread jam on top. Fold to make 16x5-inch rectangle; seal edges. Cut crosswise into 1-inch strips. Loosely twist each; arrange in greased 11x7x1½-inch baking dish. Melt remaining butter; brush over twists. Cover; let rise till double (about 1¼ hours). Bake at 375° for 15 to 20 minutes. Makes 16.

Lemon Puff Pillow Buns

3¼ cups sifted all-purpose flour
1 package active dry yeast
¾ cup milk
6 tablespoons butter or margarine
¼ cup sugar
2 eggs
1 teaspoon grated lemon peel
4 3-ounce packages cream cheese, softened
3 tablespoons sugar
1 egg yolk
1 teaspoon vanilla
1 beaten egg white

In large mixer bowl combine 1½ *cups* of the flour and yeast. In saucepan heat milk, butter, ¼ cup sugar, and 1 teaspoon salt just till warm (115-120°), stirring to melt butter. Add to dry mixture; add 2 eggs and lemon peel. Beat at low speed with electric mixer for ½ minute, scraping sides of bowl. Beat 3 minutes at high speed. By hand, stir in remaining flour. Cover bowl; refrigerate at least 4 hours.

When ready to shape, blend together cream cheese, 3 tablespoons sugar, egg yolk, and vanilla. Divide dough in fourths. On generously floured surface, roll each portion into a 12x8-inch rectangle. (Keep remaining dough refrigerated.) With floured knife cut in six 4-inch squares. Place about 1 tablespoon cream cheese mixture in the center of each; bring opposite corners to the center and pinch to seal. Place 2 inches apart on a greased baking sheet. Brush with beaten egg white. Let rise, *uncovered*, in warm place till half again as large, not double (20 to 30 minutes). Bake at 400° till done, about 10 minutes. Serve hot. Makes 24.

Chocolate-Orange Rolls

2½ cups sifted all-purpose flour
1 package active dry yeast
½ cup milk
¼ cup sugar
2 tablespoons butter or margarine
½ teaspoon salt
2 eggs
2 tablespoons butter, softened
¼ cup sugar
1 tablespoon shredded orange peel
½ cup semisweet chocolate pieces

Combine 1½ *cups* flour and yeast. In saucepan heat milk, ¼ cup sugar, 2 tablespoons butter, and salt till warm (115-120°), stirring to melt butter. Add to dry mixture; add eggs. Beat at low speed with electric mixer for ½ minute, scraping bowl. Beat 3 minutes at high speed. By hand, stir in enough remaining flour to make a moderately soft dough.

Turn out onto lightly floured surface; knead till smooth and elastic (4 to 5 minutes). Place in lightly greased bowl; turn once. Cover; let rise in warm place till double (about 1 hour). Punch down; cover and let rest 10 minutes. Roll dough to 15x10-inch rectangle. Spread with 2 tablespoons softened butter. Combine ¼ cup sugar and shredded orange peel. Sprinkle dough with sugar mixture, then with semisweet chocolate pieces. Roll up jelly-roll fashion, starting with long side. Cut roll into 18 slices; place 9 slices, cut side down, in each of two greased 9x9x2-inch baking pans. Let dough rise in warm place till nearly double (25 to 30 minutes). Bake at 375° for 12 to 15 minutes. Remove from pans and cool. Makes 18.

SWEET-SOUR—The flavor combination produced in appetizers, salads, and main dishes by blending sweet ingredients and tart ingredients in the same sauce. Neither a sweet nor a sour taste should dominate, but both should be detected.

This type of flavor blend is used by people around the world. For example, the Chinese make use of it in their sweet and sour pork dishes. The Germans like it in red cabbage dishes. And, in America, the sweet-sour flavor is equally delicious with pork, beef, poultry, and seafood dishes.

Sweet and Sour Chops

      6 pork chops, ¾ inch thick
      1 16-ounce can fruit cocktail
      3 tablespoons vinegar
      3 tablespoons brown sugar
      1 tablespoon cornstarch
      1 teaspoon instant, minced onion
    ¼ teaspoon dried dillweed

Brown chops; pour off excess fat. Drain fruit, reserving syrup. Add remaining ingredients and ½ teaspoon salt to syrup; pour over chops. Cook, covered, over low heat till tender, 30 minutes; turn chops once or twice. Remove meat. Stir fruit into sauce; heat. Spoon some sauce over chops; pass remainder. Serves 6.

Sweet-Sour Burgers

      1 8-ounce can tomato sauce (1 cup)
      6 gingersnaps, crushed (⅓ cup)
    ⅓ cup finely chopped onion
    ¼ cup raisins
      1 beaten egg
   1½ pounds ground beef
      2 tablespoons brown sugar
      1 tablespoon vinegar
      1 teaspoon prepared mustard

Combine ¼ *cup* of the tomato sauce, the gingersnaps, onion, raisins, egg, and ¾ teaspoon salt. Add meat; mix well. Shape into six patties; brown in skillet. Combine the remaining tomato sauce, the brown sugar, vinegar, mustard, and dash pepper. Pour over burgers. Cover and simmer 20 minutes, spooning sauce over the burgers occasionally. Makes 6 servings.

Sweet-Sour Spareribs

      4 pounds pork spareribs, cut in
          serving-sized pieces
      1 20½-ounce can pineapple tidbits
    ⅓ cup chopped celery
    ⅓ cup chopped green pepper
      2 tablespoons butter or margarine
      2 tablespoons cornstarch
      1 clove garlic, minced
    ⅓ cup vinegar
      2 tablespoons soy sauce
      1 tablespoon sugar
    ½ teaspoon ground ginger

Place ribs, meaty side down, in shallow roasting pan. Season with salt and pepper. Roast at 450° for 30 minutes. Drain off excess fat. Turn ribs meaty side up. Reduce oven temperature to 350° and continue roasting 1 hour.

Meanwhile, drain pineapple, reserving syrup. In saucepan cook celery and green pepper in butter till tender. Combine cornstarch and reserved pineapple syrup. Add to saucepan; cook and stir till mixture thickens and bubbles. Stir in pineapple, garlic, vinegar, soy sauce, sugar, ginger, and ½ teaspoon salt; pour over ribs. Roast till tender, about 30 minutes, basting occasionally. Serves 4 to 6.

Sweet-Sour Tuna

In medium saucepan combine one 10½-ounce can chicken gravy, ¼ cup sugar, 2 tablespoons vinegar, and 2 tablespoons soy sauce. Add 1 medium green pepper, cut in ¾-inch squares. Bring to boiling; cover and simmer for 8 minutes, stirring mixture occasionally.

Add one 13½-ounce can pineapple tidbits, drained (1 cup), and one 9¼-ounce can tuna, drained and broken into chunks. Cook till tuna and pineapple are heated through, about 2 minutes longer. Serve the mixture over one 3-ounce can chow mein noodles *or* 2 cups hot, cooked rice. Makes 4 servings.

A tropical feast

Meaty Sweet-Sour Spareribs have the sweet- →
ness of pineapple and the tartness of vinegar
with just a hint of ground ginger.

SWISS CHARD—An alternate name for the vegetable, chard. (See also *Chard.*)

SWISS CHEESE—A firm, ripened cheese also called Emmental or Emmentaler. The holes or eyes throughout the pale yellow cheese are one of the most outstanding characteristics of Swiss cheese, making it readily recognizable. Flavorwise, it has a nutty, sweet, mild taste. The texture of Swiss is smooth and elastic.

Swiss (Emmentaler) cheese was originally made in Bern, Switzerland, some time during the mid 1400s. Since Bern is in the Emmental Valley, the cheese was named after its place of origin.

Cheesemaking techniques in early years were primitive compared with today's modern processes. Wood fires supplied heat for preparing the cheese, while pine branches cut up the curd. The resulting product was a Swiss cheese without holes, unlike today's product. It was a durable cheese and frequently was transported great distances.

In the mid-1800s, Swiss immigrants brought their cheesemaking skills to America, where many of them settled in Wisconsin. Much of the American Swiss Cheese is produced in Wisconsin today. Swiss cheese is also made in Illinois, Idaho, Minnesota, Ohio, Utah, and Wyoming. Other producers of a Swiss-type cheese are France, Denmark, Germany, Italy, Austria, and Finland.

How Swiss cheese is produced: Natural Swiss cheese is made either in the traditional wheels having a rind, or in rindless rectangular blocks. Both are made from partially skimmed milk, which is clarified and may be pasteurized; likewise, the fat content is adjusted so that the milk contains the required amount of fat. A starter of bacteria cultures is used, one of which is largely responsible for the development of the holes and the characteristic flavor. A rennet extract is added to aid curd (soft lumps) formation. The curd is mixed and cut with a Swiss cheese harp into small pieces about the size of a wheat kernel. After this, the pieces are stirred and heated. However, from here on the processes vary.

Swiss cheese is easily identified by its holes.

To make the traditional wheel of Swiss cheese, the whey (watery liquid) is drained and pressed from the curd. The pressed curd, shaped in a large, flat round piece, is then salted in a brine for two to three days. After the salting process, the cheese is placed in a cold room where it is washed, turned, and rubbed daily with salt for 7 to 10 days. The next step is the ripening process, which takes place in a warm room. During this time the eyes begin to form. The last step is a slower curing of the cheese in a cold room where the cheese is stored. Minimum curing of Swiss cheese in the United States is two months; however, most of the cheese sold has been cured three to four months. Swiss from Switzerland is cured 6 to 10 months, giving it a stronger flavor.

On the other hand, for rindless Swiss cheese, an American innovation, the mixture is prepared as for the other kind then, after cooking, the curd and whey are pumped into a vat where the curd settles out. After the whey is drained off, the curd is pressed and cut into blocks. The cheese is then salted in a brine, dried, wrapped in plastic wrap, and put into a box to cure. It, too, is kept at specified cool and warm temperatures for curing.

Another Swiss cheese product available, pasteurized process Swiss cheese is prepared by grinding or cutting up fresh and aged natural Swiss cheese, applying heat, and adding an emulsifying agent. The heating (pasteurization) stops any action of bacteria, consequently there is no further ripening and no further change in flavor. This type of cheese has longer keeping qualities and melts more easily than natural cheese.

Nutritional value: Swiss cheese contains the nutrients of milk, adding protein, fat, calcium, phosphorus, and vitamin A to the diet. One ounce of Swiss cheese contributes about 100 calories.

How to buy: Both domestic and imported natural Swiss cheese are available in many markets. Swiss cheese is frequently found prepackaged in pieces and slices. In some specialty cheese stores, you can buy a piece off of a large wheel of natural cheese. To aid in your selection, some retailers will offer you a sample of cheese.

How to store: Keep Swiss cheese in the refrigerator, tightly covered to prevent it from drying out. When you are ready to eat the cheese, cut off the amount to serve and let it come to room temperature.

For longer storage, Swiss cheese can be frozen, although there may be a change in texture. Quickly freeze in small pieces of about eight ounces. Wrap and seal tightly. When ready to use, slowly thaw cheese in the refrigerator while it is still wrapped. If you are planning to shred the cheese, it's easier to do when the piece is still partially frozen. Cheese that has been frozen tends to crumble and be dry, so it is not at its best for slicing, although it is fine for cooked dishes.

How to use: Swiss cheese is a very versatile cheese and has many uses. For snacks or appetizers, simply cut the cheese in cubes or chunks and spear with wooden picks. Or shred and sprinkle Swiss cheese over vegetables or main dishes; use as an ingredient in baked main dishes, such as a soufflé; or combine in a salad. Probably Swiss cheese is most frequently used in sandwiches, especially the popular combination, ham and cheese on rye bread. Cheese fondue is also typically made with Swiss cheese. (See also *Cheese.*)

Instead of pie for dessert, prepare Swiss Pie for a leisurely brunch. The shell is made with buttered cracker crumbs and the filling contains Swiss cheese, bacon, onion, and sour cream.

Swiss Pie

Serve pie for the main dish—

Combine 1 cup finely crushed saltine cracker crumbs (28 crackers) and ¼ cup butter or margarine, melted. Press crumb mixture onto bottom and sides of an 8-inch pie plate.

Cook 6 slices bacon till crisp. Drain bacon and crumble. Pour off all but 2 tablespoons of the bacon drippings. Add 1 cup chopped onion to reserved drippings and cook till tender but not brown. Combine crumbled bacon; cooked onion; 8 ounces natural Swiss cheese, shredded (2 cups); 2 slightly beaten eggs; ¾ cup dairy sour cream; ½ teaspoon salt; and dash pepper. Pour mixture into prepared pie shell. Sprinkle 2 ounces sharp process American cheese, shredded (½ cup), atop the mixture.

Bake at 375° till knife inserted off-center comes out clean, about 25 to 30 minutes. Let pie stand 5 to 10 minutes before cutting into wedges. Makes 4 to 6 servings.

Swiss Cheese-Egg Bake

- 6 hard-cooked eggs, sliced
- 6 ounces process Swiss cheese, shredded (1½ cups)
- 1 10½-ounce can condensed cream of chicken soup
- ¾ cup milk
- ½ teaspoon prepared mustard
- 6 slices buttered French bread, ½ inch thick

Reserve 6 egg slices for garnish. Place remaining egg slices in bottom of 10x6x1¾-inch baking dish or 1½-quart casserole. Sprinkle eggs with shredded cheese. In a saucepan mix soup, milk, and mustard; heat, stirring till smooth. Pour sauce over eggs, being sure some sauce goes to bottom of dish. Place buttered bread slices on top, overlapping slightly. Bake at 350° till heated through, about 35 minutes. Garnish with reserved egg slices. Sprinkle with paprika, if desired. Serves 6.

Creamed eggs take on a different twist when baked in the oven with a Swiss cheese sauce that starts with canned soup. Swiss Cheese-Egg Bake makes a perfect Sunday night supper dish.

Ham–Asparagus Broil

Sandwiches with a Swiss cheese topper—

1 10-ounce package frozen
    asparagus spears
2 teaspoons prepared mustard
4 slices white bread, toasted
4 slices boiled ham
2 ounces process Swiss cheese,
    shredded (½ cup)
2 tablespoons chopped green onion
1 tablespoon chopped, canned
    pimiento

Cook asparagus according to package directions; drain and keep warm. Spread mustard on one side of each slice toast. Place ham slices on bread. Arrange hot asparagus atop ham. Toss together cheese, green onion, and pimiento. Sprinkle cheese mixture over asparagus. Broil sandwiches 5 inches from heat till cheese melts, about 2 to 3 minutes. Makes 4.

Buttermilk Fondue

2 tablespoons cornstarch
    Dash ground nutmeg
1 pound natural Swiss cheese,
    shredded (4 cups)
2 cups buttermilk
    French bread dippers

In bowl combine cornstarch, ½ teaspoon salt, nutmeg, and dash pepper. Toss cheese with cornstarch mixture. In saucepan carefully heat buttermilk. When warm, gradually add cheese; stir constantly till cheese melts and mixture thickens. Transfer to fondue pot; place over fondue burner. Spear dipper with fondue fork; dip in fondue, swirling to coat. Serves 6 to 8.

SWISS STEAK—A meat dish prepared by braising a less tender cut of meat, usually beef round or chuck steak. Veal is occasionally used in place of the beef.

Fork tender, Pizza Swiss Steak, is smothered with a tomato sauce-pizza sauce blend. Oregano, the herb familiar to pizza fans, adds additional flavor to this family main dish.

Before the meat is cooked, it is prepared by pounding into it a seasoned flour mixture, using a meat mallet or other suitable utensil. The pounding helps tenderize the meat. The next step calls for browning the meat slowly on all sides in a small amount of hot shortening. The meat may be cooked in one large piece or cut into serving-sized pieces.

Liquid, such as tomatoes or bouillon, is added, and the meat is baked in the oven or simmered slowly on the top of the range until the meat is tender. Other vegetables, such as onion, celery, carrot, and green pepper may be added for flavor.

Oven Swiss Steak

A main dish for two—

> ½ to ¾ pound boneless beef
>   round steak, ¾ inch thick
> 2 tablespoons all-purpose flour
> ½ teaspoon salt
>   Shortening
> 1 8-ounce can stewed tomatoes
>   (1 cup)
> ¼ cup chopped celery
> ¼ cup chopped carrot
> 1 tablespoon chopped onion
> ¼ teaspoon Worcestershire sauce
> 2 tablespoons shredded sharp
>   process American cheese

Cut meat into 2 portions. Mix flour and salt; pound into meat. Set aside remaining flour. Brown meat in small amount of hot shortening. Place meat in small, shallow baking dish. Blend remaining flour with drippings in skillet. Add remaining ingredients, except cheese; cook, stirring constantly, till mixture boils. Pour over meat. Cover and bake at 350° till meat and vegetables are tender, about 2 hours. Sprinkle cheese over meat. Return to oven for few minutes to melt cheese. Makes 2 servings.

Swiss steak topped with cheese

← Prepare an oven meal featuring Oven Swiss Steak and baked potatoes. For the salad, toss together lettuce, oranges, and avocado slices.

Swiss Steak

> ¼ cup all-purpose flour
> 1 teaspoon salt
> ¼ teaspoon pepper
> 2 pounds beef round steak, 1
>   inch thick
> 3 tablespoons shortening
> ½ cup chopped onion
> 1 16-ounce can tomatoes, cut up
> 2 tablespoons chopped green
>   pepper

Combine flour, 1 teaspoon salt, and ¼ teaspoon pepper; pound into meat. In large skillet brown meat on both sides in hot shortening.* Top with onion and tomatoes. Cover; cook over low heat till tender, about 1½ hours. Add green pepper; cook 15 minutes more. Skim off excess fat. Thicken juices, if desired. Season to taste. Makes 6 to 8 servings.

*To oven bake, transfer browned meat to 11¾x7½x1¾-inch baking dish. Top with onion and tomatoes. Bake, covered, at 350° for 1½ hours. Uncover; add green pepper and bake 15 minutes more, basting meat occasionally.

Pizza Swiss Steak

> 2 pounds beef round steak,
>   1 inch thick
> 2 tablespoons all-purpose flour
> 2 teaspoons salt
> ¼ teaspoon pepper
> 3 tablespoons shortening
>   •   •   •
> 1 8-ounce can tomato sauce
> 1 8-ounce can pizza sauce
> ½ cup water
> ½ teaspoon dried oregano leaves,
>   crushed
> ½ teaspoon sugar
> 1 medium onion, sliced

Cut meat into 6 serving-sized pieces. Combine flour, salt, and pepper; pound into steak. In skillet brown meat slowly on both sides in hot shortening. Transfer to 11¾x7½x1¾-inch baking dish. Combine tomato sauce, pizza sauce, water, oregano, and sugar. Pour sauce over meat. Top with onion slices. Cover and bake at 350° for 1 hour. Uncover; bake till tender, about 30 minutes longer. Serves 6 to 8.

SWORDFISH—A large, lean, saltwater fish living in both the Atlantic and Pacific oceans. During the summer months, most of the fish is caught along the New England and mid-Atlantic coast. The best swordfishing along the Pacific coast occurs during the early winter. Swordfish are also found in waters all over the world, including the Mediterranean Sea.

The swordfish looks like an oversized mackerel and has a double-edge sword, measuring three to five feet long, that juts out in front. The sword is used to kill or injure its prey as the fish swings it about. The tail of the swordfish is crescent shaped, making it possible for the fish to move rapidly in the water.

The average fish weighs several hundred pounds, and the usual market size is between 50 and 200 pounds. Unfortunately, swordfish has become the victim of mercury pollution and temporarily has been removed from the United States market. (See also *Fish.*)

SYLLABUB, SILLABUB *(sil' uh bub')*—An old-fashioned English drink made of sweetened milk and wine or cider. Today's version is a frothy drink similar to eggnog. If thick, it can be eaten with a spoon as a dessert, or used as a topping.

Syllabub

2 cups dry white wine
2 teaspoons grated lemon peel
¼ cup lemon juice
• • •
1¼ cups sugar
3 cups milk
2 cups light cream
4 egg whites
Ground nutmeg

In large bowl combine wine, lemon peel, and lemon juice. Add ¾ *cup* of the sugar, stirring till sugar dissolves. Add milk and cream; beat with rotary beater till frothy. Beat egg whites till soft peaks form; gradually add remaining ½ cup sugar, beating till whites stand in peaks. Pour wine mixture into punch bowl; top with puffs of egg white and sprinkle egg whites with ground nutmeg. Makes about 8 cups.

SYNERESIS *(si ner' i sis)*—The technical word used when liquid separates or waters out of certain foods. This problem is sometimes referred to as weeping. Examples of syneresis or weeping occur in jellies that have a high acid content. Another example is found in egg custards cooked at too high a temperature or for too long. The overcooking causes the custard to curdle or separate.

SYRUP, SIRUP—1. A solution of sugar and liquid used for sweetening. These sugar syrups may or may not be flavored. 2. A sweet, viscous liquid, such as cane syrup and molasses prepared from sugar cane; sorghum syrup from sorghum cane; maple syrup from the sap of maple trees; corn syrup—both light and dark—from cornstarch; and honey, one of the oldest syrups, produced from the nectar of flowers by honeybees. All of these syrups are pourable and usually are rather sticky. Other prepared syrups include chocolate and fruit-flavored syrups.

Nutritional value: Since most syrups are mainly carbohydrate, their primary contribution to the diet is to supply energy, in addition to adding a sweet flavor. Most syrups also contain small amounts of vitamins and minerals. Caloriewise, one tablespoon of maple syrup or molasses has about 50 calories, one tablespoon of corn syrup has 57 calories, and one tablespoon of honey adds 64 calories to the diet. One tablespoon of chocolate-flavored syrup has 49 calories.

How to prepare and use: Sugar syrups are prepared by cooking sugar and liquid (usually water) together in varying proportions until the sugar crystals are dissolved and the mixture thickens to the desired consistency or concentration. The concentration of the syrup depends both on how much sugar is used and how long the mixture is cooked. These sugar syrups are used in canning and freezing, in beverages, desserts, and candies.

One important use for plain sugar syrups is in preparation of fruit for canning and freezing. Most fruits are frozen or canned in a medium syrup. However, some tart varieties, such as sour cherries, need a heavier syrup, while other fruits, such as melons or apples, are best when prepared with a thin syrup. If you prefer a less sweet fruit, use a thin syrup.

Another use for plain sugar syrups is in the sweetening of cold beverages and fruits which are eaten for desserts. Since sugar doesn't dissolve as well when mixed with cold liquid, a cooked sugar solution, called simple syrup, is frequently used to add sweetness. Prepare simple syrup by simply boiling together equal amounts of sugar and water, or two parts sugar and one part water. The mixture can be kept on hand in a covered jar in the refrigerator and used as needed. The advantage of using the cooked syrup is that all the sugar is dissolved.

Sugar syrups used for candies and cooked frostings must be cooked to the exact concentration for the desired texture of the finished product. The best test for doneness when preparing syrup for candies or cooked frostings is a candy thermometer, or the cold water test. (See also *Candy*.)

Syrup is the name given also to sugar solutions flavored with chocolate and various types of fruit. These flavored syrups are then used in beverages or as ice cream, dessert, and waffle toppers.

Commercially prepared syrups, including honey and corn syrup, are often ingredients in recipes. Fruits and spices are blended with these ingredients, making them flavorful sauces for ice cream.

Many of the prepared syrups can be used as they come from the bottle. For example, maple syrup or molasses on waffles or French toast are popular combinations.

Cinnamon-Cream Syrup

   1 cup sugar
   ½ cup light corn syrup
   ¼ cup water
   ½ to ¾ teaspoon ground cinnamon
   ½ cup evaporated milk

In small saucepan combine sugar, corn syrup, water, and cinnamon. Bring to boiling over medium heat, stirring constantly. Cook and stir 2 minutes longer. Remove from heat and cool 5 minutes. Stir in evaporated milk. Serve warm over pancakes or waffles. Makes 1⅔ cups.

Honey-Citrus Syrup

   ½ cup honey
   ½ cup light corn syrup
   1 teaspoon grated orange peel
   ¼ cup orange juice
   2 teaspoons lemon juice

In a saucepan combine honey, corn syrup, orange peel, orange juice, and lemon juice. Bring mixture to boiling. Reduce heat and simmer 5 minutes. Cool and serve the syrup over French toast. Makes 1 cup syrup.

Berry Syrup

Quick and easy to prepare—

   1 10-ounce package frozen, sliced
      strawberries, thawed, *or* 1 16-
      ounce can blueberries
   ½ cup light corn syrup
      Dash salt

With electric blender or mixer blend strawberries or blueberries till smooth. In a saucepan combine the blended berries, corn syrup, and salt. Bring to boiling; boil gently, stirring constantly, till consistency of syrup, about 5 minutes. Serve warm over pancakes or waffles. Makes 1½ to 2 cups.

Sugar syrups

Combine sugar and water together in a saucepan and boil for 5 minutes.

	Simple Syrup	Thin Syrup	Medium Syrup	Heavy Syrup
Sugar (cups)	2	2	3	4¾
Water (cups)	1 to 2	4	4	4
Yield (cups)	2 to 3	5	5½	6½

T

TABLE D'HÔTE *(tab' uhl dōt')* — A French phrase found on restaurant menus indicating all the courses of a meal at one set price. It is the opposite of *à la carte*.

TABLE SETTINGS — Most homemakers today prepare and serve approximately one thousand meals during the course of a year. However routine this may sound, it can be an enjoyable part of caring for your family, and entertaining some friends and relatives occasionally. It does take creativity to set the table with care and attention so that it has eye appeal, and to vary the menu so that meals are not monotonous, but it is well worth the extra effort that goes into it.

A skillful combination of scale, proportion, and color are the three basic ingredients that make a dinner, luncheon, or buffet table a pleasure to behold. The table, centerpiece, china, crystal, and linens should all be scaled to the size of the dining area and should be in proportion to each other. For example, candles should be compatible with the height of the crystal and centerpiece. But above all, color is the most important key.

When one thinks of table settings, a person is most apt to think of dinnerware first. But, glass came into being long before either china or silver. Actually, it was an accidental discovery. Glass is made from sand and soda ash fused into liquid with intense heat, and then hardened. Museums have small opalescent glass bottles that date back to 700 B.C. The glass blowing method was not discovered until much later. From then on, it was an important part in the economy of the Roman Empire, and it spread through Europe.

Although dinnerware is commonly referred to as "china," it is really a term that covers china and porcelain pottery, earthenware, stoneware, and plastic.

China gained its name from the country of its origin. For a long time, the process of making it was carefully guarded by the Orientals who developed it. Later, the manufacture of china was introduced in England, France, Germany, Finland, and the United States. The mixture of clays and stone and the extremely high temperatures at which they are fired result in the fine quality of china or porcelain. China has long been and still is the strongest dinnerware made. It will with-

Formal table setting

← These graceful table appointments are conducive to stimulating conversation when entertaining at an evening dinner party.

stand hard wear, and even though it may get chipped or cracked, it will not absorb any moisture. It has a transluscent quality that pottery and earthenware lack.

Pottery can be traced back thousands of years. At first, the drying out process was done by the sun, later in an open fire, and finally in an oven. Another step forward occurred when it was discovered that covering the clay surface with sand before firing produced a harder surface. Pottery is still one of our most popular materials and over the years, countries have developed patterns, shapes, and designs of their own.

Earthenware is a more refined type of pottery. Finer clays are used, and they are fired at a higher temperature than pottery, but a lower temperature and for a shorter time than China. Ironstone, stoneware, and stone china are all different types of earthenware.

Plastic dinnerware is a recent entry on the market, but its widespread acceptance is due to the fact that it resists chipping, breaking, and cracking.

The history of silverware, or flatware, goes back thousands of years. At one time, primitive men used shells for eating. Later, they added wooden or bone handles to the shells and the spoon was born. The knife began as a clumsy stone instrument, at first used only for hunting, then, during the Middle Ages for both hunting and eating. The fork was well known as a weapon, especially because of its association with the Devil himself. Around the year 1400, people carried their own eating utensils with them. From one- to two-hundred years later, it became the custom to see the knives, forks, and spoons a part of the table setting. In ancient times, flatware was made of precious metals such as bronze, gold, or sterling silver. More recently, silverplate and stainless steel have gained a big share of the market.

Tablecloths have been referred to as far back in history as Biblical times. They expressed quality, luxury, and social position. Often, the cloth was artistically draped. Using fingers for eating was such

For a traditional, semiformal dinner, place silver as you use it from outside to inside. Bread and butter plate is optional, water glass goes above knife, and wine glass to the right.

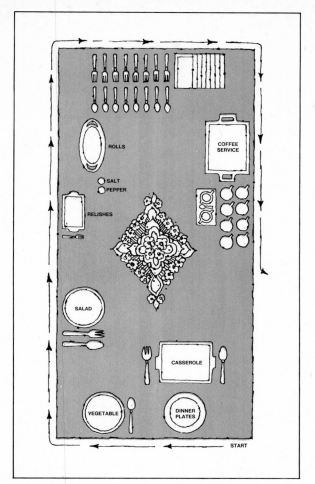

When setting a buffet table, it is important that guests can serve themselves in logical sequence. At one end of table, arrange dinner plates and main course. Arrange silverware and napkins so they are picked up last.

When serving English-style, the setting is semiformal. The main dishes are served at the table by the host, then the plates are passed to the guests. The pieces indicated by the dotted lines are considered optional.

an accepted procedure in those days that napkins were even more essential than they are in present times. They were generous in size and rectangularly shaped. Both tablecloths and napkins were folded with special care.

When there was political unrest during medieval times, it was not at all uncommon for all the guests to be seated on one side of the table with their backs to the wall. This seating arrangement was designed to eliminate the possibility of assassins approaching from the rear.

Traditional table settings: Although a great deal of today's entertaining is informal, there are occasions when formal table settings are in order. These are the times when you get out your best china, polish the silver, and use your finest crystal and table linens. Don't forget to add a centerpiece and glowing tapers.

The rules for setting a table are the same as they have been for centuries. The forks are placed on the left, with knives and spoons on the right, all placed from the outside in, in order of use.

The knife blade always should face the plate, with the spoon to the right of the knife. The napkin should be placed beside and to the left of the forks.

Place the plate and silverware about one inch from the table edge and space the settings about 15 inches apart. Glasses should be placed above the knife; wine glasses, above the spoons.

The same rules apply for a luncheon as for a dinner except that the smaller luncheon plates are used. If coffee is served during the meal, the cup and saucer should be placed just outside the top edge of the teaspoon. Two teaspoons should be set if the dessert you serve requires a spoon. You may place the second spoon on the dessert plate.

If one or more of your guests are left-handed, you might arrange to seat them where they will not be bumping elbows with the person seated next to them.

Cardinal red geraniums twining around a pair of mushroom candy jars make a striking centerpiece for a sophisticated table setting done in black, white, and silver.

The choice of the table cover is determined by the formality of the occasion. For a traditional semiformal dinner, it could be damask, fine Madeira, or imported linen. There should be an overhang of from 10 to 15 inches. Dinner napkins should not be less than 18 inches square and, for formal affairs, should be 24 inches square. For luncheon service, 15 inches square is sufficient. The formal dinner napkin should be folded in thirds to form a rectangle, preferably not longer than the diameter of the service plate. For informal settings, such as a brunch, luncheon, or an afternoon tea, the triangular fold is often used. The longest side of the napkin should be placed next to the forks. The oblong fold is also used for luncheons and buffets. The most important rule of table setting is that all table linens must be immaculately pressed. This is not the chore that it once was, as fabrics have permanent press qualities, even fine table linens.

To continue the traditional theme, you will probably want to use flowers and

A centerpiece that is a structural triumph of Lucite muddlers and candle cubes holds yellow tapers and roses. The same color is repeated in the napkin on the china plate.

candles for a centerpiece. Choose colors that are compatible with your china and with the season of the year.

Contemporary table settings: For the young at heart, there is an unlimited opportunity to take whatever is at hand and make a festive occasion of it.

No longer need dinnerware be china. It can be handcrafted pottery, earthenware, even plastic. Table linens can be colorful fabrics – tablecloths, runners, place mats. Place mats can also be plastic or woven raffia or straw. Napkins need not match the table cover. They can provide sharp contrast in a solid color, a plaid, stripe, or print. Flatware may be the traditional silver, or it can be stainless in a contemporary pattern, or one of the patterns with ebony or bamboo handles.

When it comes to centerpieces, let your imagination run riot. Try a bowl of fruit or vegetables, a straw hat filled with a sheaf of wheat and dried grasses, or a compote of greens and bright berries. For a Christmas party, arrange a heap of miniature gift-wrapped packages in the middle of the table. For an individual touch, place a small nosegay at each place setting. For a futuristic theme, use clear plastic, sparkling silver, and mirrored glass that reflects the bright color scheme. Use one sharp color for candles and napkins to contrast with the see-through look. Or make a centerpiece of candles – short ones, fat ones, sculptured ones, different colors, and in an assortment of candle holders.

Look around your home and you'll probably be able to come up with all sorts of objects that will lend themselves to the arrangement of an unusual centerpiece.

Table setting extras: Have salt and pepper shakers conveniently placed – and remember to put out more than one set. If there are smokers in the group, place ashtrays where they are easy to reach.

A cloudlike centerpiece of opaque and clear crystal candlesticks and vase piled with softly packed mums complements china, silver, and frosty-leafed stemmed goblets.

A duet of canisters filled with semivisible flowers combined with a nubby Persian candlestick decorates a table with griege-flowered plates and sterling flatware.

An informal Christmas holiday dinner features Indian tree pattern earthenware, Vienna pattern sterling, and red Argus tumblers. Lanterns are surrounded by pine for the centerpiece.

Holiday table settings: Any holiday can be a gala occasion if you adapt the table settings, the decorations, and the menu to fit the specific festivity.

The holidays that come to mind most frequently are New Year's Day, St. Valentine's Day, St. Patrick's Day, April Fool's Day, Easter, Independence Day, Halloween, Thanksgiving, and Christmas. For these holidays, the decorations and the menu are established by custom.

But don't stop with this list. Why not a party for Texas Independence Day, First Day of Spring, Ground Hog Day, Bunker Hill Day, or Bastille Day? The list is endless, and many times the guests show more enthusiasm for these little-publicized holidays than they do for the more traditionally celebrated ones.

Whatever you plan to celebrate, design your decorations, flowers, and centerpiece so that they fit the theme.

For an inexpensive theme for any patriotic holiday, use these corrugated cardboard innovations. Paint cardboard blue for place mats and trim them with gold, red, white, and blue ribbon. Trim the tubes of corrugated paper with ribbon for napkin rings. The centerpiece is a coffee can covered with corrugated board, filled with strips of cardboard folded back to form an abstract flower, centered with a large, gold tree ornament.

The Easter egg tree, a symbol of new life, sets the stage for an Easter buffet. Blown and dyed eggs are hung from the limbs of a manzanita branch. Ham, a traditional entrée, is beautifully glazed and trimmed with a candied orange daisy. It is accompanied with frilly leaf-lettuce salad, asparagus with almond topping, and parslied new potatoes. Serve hot rolls and coffee and top with Easter basket desserts made of meringue shells filled with ice cream balls.

Table settings for special occasions:
Even the simplest occasion will take on added glamour if you plan the table settings and the menu so they are in tune with the event you are celebrating.

It may be that your husband has invited his boss home to dinner with only a last-minute warning. It may be that your dining space is limited. Or worse yet, it might be just before payday when your budget is almost depleted. You might get carried away and issue an impromptu invitation to friends to come home for refreshments after a football game or a theatrical production.

Whatever the occasion, approach it with confidence. Decorate your table so it presents a festive look, and serve food, regardless of whether it be simple or elegant, that looks appealing and fits the spirit of the occasion.

What could be more fun for a children's party than a treasure hunt? The table centerpiece is the padlocked treasure chest filled with prizes for everyone. Organize the young guests into teams to search for the key. The individual place mats with skull and crossbones motif enhance the pirate theme.

Hickory, dickory, dock. For the nursery rhyme set, cut a clock from a shoe box, make a paper plate face, and hang a pendulum inside. Invent "mouse" games to play. Gaily striped paper plates and cups add a colorful touch and minimize clean-up chores after the small guests have departed.

A handsomely decorated cake atop a silver pedestal tray is the centerpiece for a "Silver Anniversary Buffet." Its colors are coordinated with those of the pink and white theme. The pink tablecloth provides a perfect background for white china and silver flatware and coffee and tea service.

For an authentic south-of-the-border table setting, make candlesticks from 10c store funnels attached at each end with paper cores, sprayed silver, and trimmed with pocket mirrors outlined in fringed foil. Paper flowers are made of crepe paper and tape.

For a unique bridal kitchen shower, use a scale as a centerpiece on the buffet table. Fill one side with a colorful bouquet of flowers and the other with small kitchen gadgets—measuring spoons, cups, scoops, an appliance timer, and a candy thermometer.

You can use your kitchen for casual entertaining. In this case, white ironstone and green pottery dishes, green tumblers, and napkins are a pleasing contrast to the red and white checked tablecloth.

Casual table settings: With so many of the homes and apartments of today lacking a formal dining room, entertaining informally has become an accepted way of contemporary living. The food can be just as taste-tempting, and the table settings just as attractive as those meals served in more elegant surroundings. It doesn't matter whether you serve in a dining alcove at one end of the living room, a breakfast area in the kitchen, on individual trays, or buffet style.

This type of entertaining offers the hostess a wonderful opportunity to use her most colorful linens, dishes and crystal—and to create unusual centerpieces. And you don't have to have complete sets of everything to match. Some of the most interesting table settings combine several colors, patterns, and textures. You can also deviate from the traditional silverware and napkin placement if you are in the mood to try something different. Table decorations—flowers, candles, and centerpieces—can be adapted to the more informal theme, too.

This is the ideal time for you to use oven-to-table cookware rather than the conventional serving dishes. Or, you may

Greek key pattern tracing the rim of this white china is teamed with black, white, red, and blue for a Mediterranean atmosphere. Napkin color contrasts with place mats for a striking arrangement of opposites.

Creative silverware placement can add a touch of flair to a casual table setting. The knife, fork, and spoon on the plate of daisies below crisscross in contrast to the nubby-textured place mats with stripes.

choose to try tabletop cooking. Fondue and chafing dish meals are a boon to to-day's busy homemaker, as well as fun for the guests who participate. Other cook-at-the-table units include electric skillets and griddles and the less familiar porta-ble ovens and burners that are equally handy. There are also special servers that keep foods hot or cold.

Outdoor table decorations: The great outdoors offers unlimited themes for un-usual table settings. It doesn't matter whether your style tends to run toward garden, patio, porch, or poolside enter-taining; or whether you are the type who prefers a picnic in the woods, on the bank of a river, at the beach, or on the tailgate of the family station wagon. Serve food that will appease ravenous appetites that are whetted by the fresh outdoor air and sunshine, and use tableware that fairly sings with brilliant color.

There are disposable dishes, tumblers, tablecloths, place mats, and napkins in a wide variety of colors, designs, and themes. Even throwaway knives, forks, and spoons of brightly colored plastic minimize clean-up chores still further.

If you desire a little more formality, use plastic dishes whose designs simu-late some of the finest dinnerware pat-terns, and plastic goblets that resemble crystal. Stainless steel flatware, and handcrafted place mats with matching or contrasting napkins complete the theme.

If you have an irresistible urge to do a complete about-face, why not give a formal picnic? Spread out your finest linen tablecloth on the lawn (protected from the moisture underneath with a sheet of plastic). Use your finest china, silver candelabra and flatware, sparkling crystal, and serve elegant food accom-panied by bubbling champagne.

There are only a few suggestions for outdoor entertaining. Whatever you choose to do, remember to spray with in-secticide ahead of time to keep guests comfortable. Add a few extra touches — special lighting and outdoor floral ar-rangements, as well as table centerpieces. Don't forget to place baskets in conve-nient spots for the easy disposal of litter.

You can carry out the colors in your own garden in the scheme of your table settings. Here, some of the flowers appear in a center-piece, and the same shade of red is repeated in napkins and table covering.

White, shades of blue, and deep purple are combined in table settings for an outdoor luncheon. The centerpiece of a garland of flowers and ceramic birds rests gracefully on the round wrought iron table with glass top.

TACO *(tä' kō)*—The Mexican version of a sandwich, consisting of a soft or crisp tortilla that is filled with one or more foods such as ground meat, chili peppers, cheese, or a saucy mixture. The American adaptations of crisp tacos contain spicy ground meat, shredded cheese, chopped tomato, shredded lettuce, and sometimes beans. (See also *Mexican Cookery*.)

Fish Portions, Taco-Style

    12 frozen, fried, breaded fish portions
    12 tortillas (frozen or canned)
       Shortening
    1½ cups finely shredded lettuce
    12 thin tomato slices
     6 ounces natural Cheddar cheese,
          shredded (1½ cups)
       Bottled taco sauce

Cook fish portions according to package directions. Meanwhile, heat ¼ inch shortening in skillet. Fry tortillas till lightly browned. Drain on paper toweling. Place one cooked fish portion on *each* tortilla; top with lettuce, tomato slice, and shredded Cheddar cheese. Serve with bottled taco sauce. Makes 6 servings.

Beef Tacos

     1 pound ground beef
     ½ cup chopped onion
     1 clove garlic, minced
     ½ teaspoon salt
     ½ teaspoon chili powder
    12 tortillas (frozen or canned)
       Shortening
     2 tomatoes, chopped and drained
     3 cups finely shredded lettuce
     8 ounces natural Cheddar cheese,
          shredded (2 cups)
       Canned Mexican hot sauce *or*
          canned enchilada sauce

Make your own tacos

← Señoritas and señors help themselves to beef, tomato, cheese, lettuce, and taco sauce as desired to make their Beef Tacos.

In skillet cook beef, onion, and garlic till meat is browned. Drain. Add salt and chili powder. Set aside; keep warm.

In skillet fry tortillas, one at a time, in ¼ inch hot shortening. When tortilla becomes limp, fold in half and hold edges apart while frying to allow for filling. Fry till crisp, 1½ to 2 minutes. Drain. Spoon about ¼ cup meat mixture into each. Top with tomato, lettuce, and cheese. Pass hot sauce. Makes 6 servings.

TAFFY—A chewy, noncrystalline candy made by boiling a blend of sugars such as granulated sugar, corn syrup, and molasses. After cooking and cooling, the thick candy mixture is pulled with buttered hands until it is light and creamy, then cut into pieces. For commercially made taffy, a machine does the pulling.

Saltwater taffy, one of the best-known types of taffy, originated at New Jersey seashore resorts. It does not contain salt water but gets its name from the oceanside origin. (See also *Candy*.)

Saltwater Taffy

     2 cups sugar
     1 cup light corn syrup
     1 cup water
    1½ teaspoons salt
              • • •
     2 tablespoons butter or margarine
     ¼ teaspoon oil of peppermint
     7 drops green food coloring

Combine sugar, corn syrup, water, and salt in a 2-quart saucepan. Cook slowly, stirring constantly, till sugar is dissolved. Continue to cook to hard-ball stage (265°) without stirring. Remove from heat; stir in remaining ingredients. Pour into buttered 15½x10½x1-inch pan. Cool till comfortable to handle.

Butter hands; gather taffy into a ball and pull.* When candy is light in color and gets hard to pull, cut in fourths; pull each piece into a long strand about ½ inch thick. With a pair of buttered scissors, quickly snip in bite-sized pieces. Wrap each piece in clear plastic wrap. Makes 1¼ pounds.

*It is best to have more than one person pulling the taffy.

TAMALE *(tuh mä' lē)*—A Mexican, Central American, and South American dish consisting of a cornmeal dough called *masa* that is wrapped around a spicy filling, then steamed in an outer wrap of corn husks or banana leaves. The variety of fillings can include highly seasoned ground chicken, beef, or pork; cheese; or sweeter ingredients such as coconut.

Tamales have been closely linked to south-of-the-border cuisines since Aztec times. According to legend, tamales saved Cortés and his men from starvation after the Spaniards' invasion of the Aztec nation that we now know as Mexico.

The characteristics of tamales differ slightly from country to country. In Peru, for example, they are more elaborate and are eaten as appetizers. American tamales are several times larger in size than their Mexican counterparts. (See also *Mexican Cookery*.)

Jiffy Mexican Dinner

¼ cup chopped onion
¼ cup chopped green pepper
1 tablespoon shortening
1 15-ounce can chili with beans

• • •

1 15-ounce can tamales in sauce
2 ounces sharp process American
cheese, shredded (½ cup)

In a 10-inch skillet cook onion and green pepper in shortening till tender. Add chili. Remove shucks from tamales; arrange spoke-fashion on top. Cook, uncovered, over low heat for 10 to 15 minutes. Sprinkle with sharp process cheese and serve. Makes 4 servings.

TAMARIND—A fruitlike seedpod of the tropical tamarind tree. The pod encloses juicy, acidic-tasting pulp and up to a dozen hard, glossy seeds.

Although native to East Africa, tamarind trees now are grown and used for food in tropical regions throughout the world. In India, the leaves and flowers as well as the fruits are eaten. The seeds are ground into a meal that is formed and baked into cakes. The fruits are well known for their use in chutneys, curries, and preserves. Tamarind juice provides the foundation for a cooling beverage.

TANGELO—A loose-skinned citrus fruit that was developed by crossing a tangerine and a grapefruit. The name is a combination of the first syllable of tangerine and the last two syllables of pomelo, the ancestral name for grapefruit. Tangelos are eaten and used like tangerines.

The four most popular varieties are Orlando, Minneola, Thornton, and Seminole. Whether tangelos are oval or round in shape or have thin, thick, rough, or smooth skins is determined by the variety. The flesh of all tangelo varieties has a unique acidic flavor reminiscent of the grapefruit. (See also *Citrus Fruit*.)

Constant pulling and twisting of the cooled Saltwater Taffy helps to give each piece its pleasing pastel color and creamy texture.

TANGERINE—A deeply colored, loose-skinned orange belonging to the mandarin family. The word tangerine is believed to have originated with a small orange variety from Tangiers, Morocco.

Tangerines are flattened on both stem and blossom ends and, like all mandarin-type oranges, have skins that are readily peeled away from the pulp. The pulp is made up of easily separated segments, each of which is just the right size for one bite. Most tangerine varieties have from one to several seeds per segment.

Nutritional value: Tangerines are as nutritious to eat as they are good-tasting. One fresh medium-sized tangerine contains only 40 calories; a cup of sweetened tangerine juice provides about 125 calories. The fruits are fair sources of vitamin C and also provide small but important amounts of vitamin A, the B vitamin complex, and assorted minerals.

How to select and store: The tangerine season is at its peak at holiday time, November through January. Perhaps that is one reason why, for generations, tangerines have been popular stuffers for the toes of Christmas stockings.

When you buy fresh tangerines, choose ones that are heavy for their size with a deep orange or reddish orange color to the peel. The skins should not feel like the pulp has shrunk away. Avoid tangerines that have pallid skin color.

Good-quality tangerines keep well when they are properly stored. Placed in the fruit-and-vegetable keeper of the refrigerator, or in perforated plastic bags and then refrigerate. Kept this way, tangerines stay fresh for several weeks.

How to use: Easy peeling and sectioning of the tangerine makes it one of the neatest of all fruits for eating out of hand or for using in recipes. The zesty fruity flavor is delicious in salads or fruit cups and in many kinds of desserts.

Tangerines also make a unique menu addition as a fruit accompaniment to pork, ham, or poultry. The candied peel makes a pleasing confection for holiday food gifts. (See also *Orange.*)

Roast Pork Tangerine

Features tangy basting sauce and gravy—

1 5- to 6-pound pork loin roast
1 teaspoon dry mustard
1 teaspoon dried marjoram leaves, crushed
1 teaspoon salt
2 teaspoons grated tangerine peel
½ cup tangerine juice
1 tablespoon brown sugar

• • •

3 tablespoons all-purpose flour
⅛ teaspoon dry mustard
Pinch dried marjoram leaves, crushed
1½ cups water
2 tangerines, peeled and sectioned

Place pork, fat side up, on rack in shallow pan. Mix the 1 teaspoon dry mustard, 1 teaspoon marjoram, and salt; rub over surface of meat. Roast at 325° for 2½ hours.

Skim most of fat from roasting pan. Combine tangerine peel, juice, and brown sugar; spoon over roast. Return to oven and roast until meat thermometer registers 170°, about 1 hour longer; baste the meat frequently.

Remove meat to platter. Pour off all but about 3 tablespoons clear fat. Blend in flour, the ⅛ teaspoon dry mustard, and pinch marjoram. Gradually add water, stirring constantly. Cook and stir till thickened and bubbly. Season to taste with salt and pepper. Just before serving, add tangerine sections to gravy. Pass with pork. Makes 10 servings.

Sunny Tangerine Creme

1 cup whipping cream
1 6-ounce can frozen tangerine juice concentrate, thawed
2 egg whites
½ cup sugar
Red food coloring

Whip cream. Fold thawed tangerine juice into whipped cream. Beat egg whites till soft peaks form; gradually add sugar, beating till stiff peaks form. Fold into cream. Tint with red food coloring. Pour into a 4-cup refrigerator tray. Freeze till firm. Makes 6 servings.

Tangerine-Walnut Toss

   1 tablespoon butter or margarine
  ½ cup broken walnuts
  ¼ teaspoon salt
   7 cups torn lettuce (about
      1 medium head)
   2 cups tangerine sections
  ½ mild white onion, sliced and
      separated in rings
  ⅓ cup Italian salad dressing
    Romaine leaves

In skillet melt butter over medium heat. Add walnuts and salt. Stir till nuts are crisp and butter browned. Toss lettuce, tangerine sections, and onion rings with Italian dressing. Line salad bowl with romaine; fill with salad. Top with walnuts. Makes 6 to 8 servings.

Tangerine-Apricot Mold

Velvety smooth texture—

   2 envelopes unflavored gelatin
      (2 tablespoons)
  ½ cup sugar
    Dash salt
1¾ cups tangerine juice*
   1 12-ounce can apricot nectar
      (1½ cups)

      • • •

   3 egg whites
  ½ cup whipping cream

Combine unflavored gelatin, sugar, salt, and tangerine juice. Cook and stir over medium heat till the gelatin dissolves. Stir in the apricot nectar; chill till the mixture is partially set. Add egg whites; beat till fluffy. Chill till partially set. Whip cream; fold into gelatin mixture. Pile into a 6½-cup mold; chill till firm. Makes 8 to 10 servings.

    *Reconstitute one 6-ounce can frozen tangerine juice concentrate; measure 1¾ cups.

Tempting winter salad

← Dark green romaine leaves accentuate pieces of tangerine, lettuce, onion, and walnut halves in Tangerine-Walnut Toss.

Tangerine-Coconut Cups

    Softened butter or margarine
   1 3½-ounce can shredded coconut,
      toasted (1⅓ cups)
   2 slightly beaten egg yolks
2½ cups milk
   1 3- or 3¼-ounce package *regular*
      vanilla pudding mix
   2 teaspoons finely grated
      tangerine peel
   3 to 4 tangerines, peeled and
      sectioned
   2 egg whites
  ¼ cup sugar

Generously butter bottoms and sides of 8 to 10 custard cups. Sprinkle with coconut; press firmly to form shells. Chill. Combine egg yolks and milk; slowly stir into pudding mix in saucepan. Cook and stir over medium heat till thickened, about 8 to 10 minutes. Add tangerine peel; cool. Set aside 8 to 10 tangerine sections for garnish. Cut up remaining sections in small pieces; fold into pudding. Spoon tangerine cream into coconut shells.

    Beat egg whites to soft peaks; gradually add sugar, beating to stiff peaks. Spread meringue over the cream-filled shells. Bake at 425° till meringue is a golden brown, 5 to 8 minutes. Cool. Garnish with reserved tangerine sections. Makes 8 to 10 servings.

Candied Tangerine Peel

   8 medium tangerines
   1 tablespoon salt
   4 cups cold water
   2 cups sugar
  ½ cup water

Cut peel of each tangerine in fourths; loosen from pulp with bowl of spoon. Add salt to the 4 cups water; add peel. Weight with a plate to keep peel under water. Let stand overnight.

    Drain; wash thoroughly. Cover with cold water; heat to boiling. Drain. Repeat 3 times.

    With kitchen scissors, cut peel in strips. In saucepan combine 2 cups cut peel, sugar, and the ½ cup water. Cook and stir till sugar dissolves. Cook slowly till peel is translucent. Drain thoroughly; roll in granulated sugar. Dry on rack. Store in covered container.

TANNIN—A substance that gives an astringent taste to foods. Some foods where tannins are most evident include fruits, nuts, coffee, tea, and red wines.

Tannins are more obvious in some fruits than others, especially when the fruit is underripe. Green bananas and unripe persimmons are good examples. If you've ever tasted a persimmon that wasn't fully ripened, you are aware of the astringent, puckery feeling that tannins give to the mouth. As the fruit ripens, the tannins become less soluble and as a result they can't give the same astringent feeling when the fruit is eaten.

Tannins do have a plus characteristic. Coffee and tea owe part of their flavor, strength, and body to tannins. However, when coffee or tea is boiled too rapidly or brewed too long, producing a strong beverage, you will notice a bitter flavor because more tannins from the coffee beans and tea leaves are dissolved.

TANSY—A garden herb with beautiful fern-like leaves. It looks prettier than it tastes, however, for it has a bitter flavor. Because of its looks, tansy is often included in home herb gardens. For generations the leaves were used in brewing herb tea, or a touch of tansy was used to flavor puddings. But this herb is seldom used in modern-day cooking.

TAPIOCA—A starch extracted from the roots of the tropical bitter cassava plant. The starch is used to thicken various cooked dishes and comes in two forms—quick-cooking and pearl tapioca.

In processing the quick-cooking type, the roots are washed, peeled, and ground to a fine pulp. The liquid, containing the starch, is drained off and the starch settles out, forming a moist cake. Tapioca flour is then made by drying and pulverizing the starch. After screening, tapioca flour is shipped to plants for further refining. First the flour is mixed with water, making a dough, which is cooked and stirred. The cooking process dries and breaks the tapioca into flakes, which are further broken down in hammer mills, then dried again, cooled, ground, and screened for uniformity of size.

Quick-cooking tapioca, as the name implies, is quick to prepare and needs no preliminary soaking. When cooked, tapioca particles become translucent. It is used in creamy milk puddings, as a thickener in fruit pie fillings and desserts, and occasionally in main dishes and soups.

The less common type of tapioca, pearl tapioca, is formed by sieving the moist starch, then processing the pellets at high temperatures. This form of tapioca must be soaked before being cooked.

Fluffy Tapioca Pudding

    1 quart milk
    ¼ cup quick-cooking tapioca
    ½ cup sugar
    ¼ teaspoon salt
    3 slightly beaten egg yolks
    1½ teaspoons vanilla
    3 stiffly beaten egg whites

In a saucepan combine milk, tapioca, sugar, and salt; let stand 5 minutes. Add egg yolks. Bring to boiling, stirring constantly. Remove from heat (mixture will be thin); add vanilla.

Put ⅓ *of beaten egg whites* in large bowl; slowly stir in tapioca mixture. Fold in remaining egg whites, leaving little "pillows" of egg white. Chill. Pile into sherbets. Garnish with tart jelly, if desired. Serves 8 to 10.

Java Tapioca Parfaits

    1 egg yolk
    ⅓ cup sugar
    2 teaspoons instant coffee powder
    2 cups milk
    3 tablespoons quick-cooking
        tapioca
    ½ teaspoon vanilla
    1 stiffly beaten egg white
    ½ cup whipping cream

In a saucepan combine egg yolk, sugar, coffee powder, milk, tapioca, and dash salt. Bring to boiling, stirring constantly. Remove from heat; add vanilla. Slowly pour hot mixture over egg white, mixing well. Cover; chill. Whip cream. Alternate layers of tapioca and whipped cream in 4 or 5 parfait glasses.

Tapioca-Cheese Soufflé

A main dish soufflé for lunch or brunch—

3 tablespoons quick-cooking
    tapioca
½ teaspoon salt
1 cup milk
3 slightly beaten egg yolks
4 ounces sharp process American
    cheese, shredded (1 cup)
¼ teaspoon Worcestershire sauce
3 stiffly beaten egg whites

In a saucepan combine tapioca, salt, and milk.
Bring to boiling, stirring constantly. Stir small
amount of hot mixture into egg yolks. Return
to hot mixture. Cook and stir over low heat
till thickened, about 1 minute. Add cheese and
Worcestershire sauce; stir till cheese melts.
Fold in egg whites. Pour into an *ungreased* 5-
cup soufflé dish. Bake at 325° till knife inserted halfway between center and edge comes
out clean, about 35 minutes. Serve the soufflé
immediately. Makes 6 servings.

Island Sweet-Sour Pork

Tapioca thickens the sauce—

1½ pounds boneless pork shoulder,
    cut in small cubes
1 tablespoon salad oil
1 teaspoon salt
    Dash pepper
1 8¾-ounce can pineapple
    tidbits
½ cup bottled barbecue sauce
1 tablespoon quick-cooking
    tapioca
    • • •
1 medium green pepper, cut in
    strips
    Hot, cooked rice

In skillet brown meat in hot oil. Season with
salt and pepper. Drain pineapple, reserving
syrup. Add water to syrup to make ¾ cup.
Stir syrup, barbecue sauce, and tapioca into
browned meat. Cover and simmer till tender,
about 45 minutes. Add drained pineapple and
green pepper; heat through. Serve over hot,
cooked rice. Makes 6 servings.

Rosy Raspberry Pie

2 10-ounce packages frozen red
    raspberries
3 tablespoons quick-cooking
    tapioca
⅔ cup sugar
    Dash salt
    Pastry for lattice-top 9-inch
    pie (See *Pastry*)

Partially defrost the frozen raspberries. In a
bowl combine tapioca, sugar, and salt; mix
with fruit and let stand 15 minutes. Spoon
berry mixture into pastry-lined pie plate.
Adjust lattice top and seal. Bake at 425° for
about 35 to 40 minutes.

TARO *(tär′ ō, târ′ ō)*—A plant with edible
rootstocks and sprouts. Taro is believed
to have originated in the Pacific islands
and was brought to the United States as
much for its ornamental quality as for
any food value it might have. As it is
quite high in starch, taro's main contribution to nutrition is energy.

Dasheen is a variety of taro and the
root of this variety is served as a vegetable. Taro is also used for puddings or it is
made into flour. The flour is used in poi,
the Hawaiian luau dish.

TARPON *(tär′ puhn)*—A large, game fish
that is found in the warm Atlantic waters
from Virginia to Brazil. It is related to the
herring, is covered with large, silvery-
looking scales, and often weighs up to
200 pounds. The fish, which has a mild
flavor, is prized by sport fishermen.

TARRAGON *(tar′ uh gon′, -guhn)*—An aromatic herb belonging to the aster family,
having a hint of licorice flavor. It is a
perennial plant with slender, pointed,
dark green leaves which may be used
fresh or dried in a variety of recipes.

Although once native to Russia, today,
tarragon is grown extensively in the
southern part of Europe, particularly in
France, and in the temperate areas of the
United States, especially California. The
herb was introduced to the United States
in the year 1806.

The tarragon purchased today is grown either in the United States or imported from Europe, especially France.

Because tarragon is very aromatic and comes through strongly, it should be used discreetly. It is one of the classic *fines herbes* and blends beautifully with tomatoes, egg dishes, fish and seafood, salads, soups, meats, and poultry. It is the basic flavor in Bearnaise Sauce and several other classic sauces, including Bordelaise and Ravigote. Tarragon is also used to flavor vinegar, and frequently used as a salad dressing ingredient.

Try fresh tarragon or a sparse sprinkling of dried leaves inside an unstuffed chicken for roasting. Or blend tarragon with butter and serve with broiled meat, poultry, or fish. (See also *Herb*.)

Herbed Chicken Salad

A main dish salad—

    1 small head romaine, torn in
        pieces (4 cups)
    2 cups cubed, cooked chicken,
        chilled
    2 tablespoons grated Parmesan
        cheese
    ½ cup salad oil
    3 tablespoons tarragon vinegar
    ½ teaspoon dry mustard
    4 drops Worcestershire sauce
        Dash pepper
    2 cups herb-seasoned stuffing
        croutons

Combine romaine, chicken, and Parmesan cheese. Mix together the oil, tarragon vinegar, dry mustard, Worcestershire sauce, and pepper. Pour *half* the dressing over the herb-seasoned croutons and toss—don't let croutons get soaked. Add the croutons to the salad with remaining dressing. Makes 8 servings.

Company best chicken

← Chicken Tarragon blends anise flavor of the herb with onions and mushrooms for a gourmet treat. Parsley adds color to the platter.

Fried Salmon Sandwich

    1 7¾-ounce can salmon
    2 well-beaten eggs
    ⅓ cup milk
        Dash ground nutmeg
    ¼ cup finely chopped celery
    ¼ cup dairy sour cream
    1 teaspoon prepared horseradish
    1 teaspoon prepared mustard
    ½ teaspoon finely chopped green
        onion
    ¼ teaspoon dried tarragon leaves,
        crushed
    ¼ teaspoon salt
    8 slices white bread
        Sesame seed
    ¼ cup shortening

Drain salmon, reserving liquid. Remove bones and skin from salmon; flake salmon into bowl. In shallow dish combine salmon liquid, eggs, milk, and nutmeg. Blend together salmon, celery, sour cream, horseradish, mustard, onion, tarragon, salt, and dash pepper. Spread mixture evenly on 4 slices bread; top with remaining 4 slices. Dip each sandwich into egg mixture; sprinkle with sesame seed. Fry in shortening on griddle till sandwiches are brown on both sides. Makes 4 sandwiches.

Chicken Tarragon

    2 teaspoons seasoned salt
    ¼ teaspoon pepper
        Dash paprika
    1 2½- to 3-pound ready-to-cook
        broiler-fryer chicken, cut up
    ¼ cup butter or margarine
    1 medium onion, thinly sliced
    1 3-ounce can sliced mushrooms,
        drained
    1 teaspoon dried tarragon leaves,
        crushed

Combine first 3 ingredients; sprinkle over chicken. Slowly brown chicken in butter; remove from pan. In same pan cook onion till tender. Move onions aside and place chicken in pan. Add mushrooms and tarragon and spoon with onions over chicken. Add ¼ cup water; cover and simmer till chicken is tender, about 30 to 40 minutes. Makes 4 servings.

TARRAGON VINEGAR—A vinegar flavored with tarragon leaves that give it a faint licorice taste. It is frequently prepared with wine vinegar, either red or white. Some vinegar products that you buy will have the tarragon leaves in them. Tarragon vinegar is especially good as one of the dressing ingredients for use in green salads. (See also *Vinegar*.)

TART—1. A descriptive word for the sour or sharp taste in foods. Lemon juice or vinegar are frequently added to foods to give them tartness. 2. A large or small pie with sweet or unsweet filling, usually prepared without a top crust.

The word tart comes from the French word, *tarte*, which refers to an open-faced pastry. To many Americans, the word brings to mind an individual pie having a pastry or crumb crust and served as an appetizer, main dish, or more frequently as a dessert. However, tarts are not limited in size to the individual serving but also can be a regular-sized, open-faced pie.

Fillings that are used for dessert tarts include custards and puddings, fruits, or jam, while main-dish and appetizer tarts are frequently filled with meat, seafood, egg, or cheese mixtures.

There are various kinds of tart shells you can use. The most common is plain or rich pastry; less common are those made with cookies or graham cracker crumbs. The preparation of tart shells takes more time than preparing one large pie. But it is worth the effort, for tarts are much easier to serve and are a welcome change from the traditional wedge of pie.

Fit the pastry into miniature pie pans or shape inside, or on the reverse side of muffin pans. Or, roll the pastry out on aluminum foil and cut out, foil and all, shape, and bake with the foil on the back (see pictures on page 2252).

Since the top crust is eliminated on most tarts, dress up the filling with a topping of whipped cream or meringue, a sprinkling of nuts, or a light dusting of ground spice. (See also *Pie*.)

Pastry for Tart Shells

For 4 to 6 tart shells:

  1½ **cups sifted all-purpose flour**
   ½ **teaspoon salt**
   ½ **cup shortening**
   4 **to 5 tablespoons cold water**

For 6 to 8 tart shells:

  2 **cups sifted all-purpose flour**
  1 **teaspoon salt**
  ⅔ **cup shortening**
  5 **to 7 tablespoons cold water**

Sift together flour and salt; cut in shortening with pastry blender or blending fork till pieces are the size of small peas. (For extra tender pastry, cut in *half* the shortening till mixture resembles cornmeal. Cut in remaining till like small peas.) Sprinkle 1 tablespoon water over part of mixture. Gently toss with fork; push to side of bowl. Sprinkle next tablespoon water over dry part; mix lightly. Push to moistened part at side. Repeat till all is moistened. Form the dough into a ball.

Flatten ball on lightly floured surface. Roll from center to edge till dough is ⅛ inch thick. Cut in 5- or 6-inch circles. Fit over inverted muffin cups or custard cups and pinch a pleat in several places. Or fit pastry in tart pans. Trim pastry ½ inch beyond edge; turn under and flute. Prick bottom and sides of pastry. Bake at 450° till golden, 10 to 12 minutes.

One way to prepare pastry tart shells is to fit pastry rounds over inverted muffin cups. Then, pinch pleats in several places.

Cran-Apple Tarts

A tart with a top crust and no bottom crust—

    1 cup cranberries, cut in half
  ½ cup sugar
    1 stick piecrust mix
    1 20-ounce can apple pie filling
  ½ teaspoon vanilla
    2 tablespoons butter or margarine

Mix berries and sugar; let stand 1 hour. Prepare piecrust mix following package directions. Roll ⅛ inch thick. Cut in 6 circles, 1 inch larger in diameter than 6-ounce custard cups. Combine pie filling, vanilla, and cranberries. Put in 6 custard cups. Dot with butter. Top with pastry. Crimp to edges of custard cups. Cut slits in tops. Bake at 425° for 25 minutes.

Frozen Mincemeat Tarts

For a change of pace at holiday time, serve this frozen mincemeat dessert—

    1 quart vanilla ice cream
    1 cup prepared mincemeat
    1 teaspoon grated orange peel
    8 baked tart shells, cooled
       • • •
    Whipped cream
    Toasted almonds

In a bowl stir ice cream just till softened. Fold in mincemeat and grated orange peel. Spoon ice cream mixture into cooled, baked tart shells. Freeze till firm. Before serving, top each tart with a dollop of whipped cream and a few toasted almonds. Makes 8 servings.

Prepare a trayful of Fresh Fruit Tarts the next time you entertain. The creamy filling is topped with assorted fresh or canned fruits so that everyone can choose his favorite.

Easy tart shells

Roll out Pastry for Tart Shells ⅛ inch thick on heavy-duty aluminum foil. Cut out 5-inch circles through pastry and foil.

Prick pastry circles with a fork. Hold pastry and foil together with foil on outside. Crimp in about five places to form shells.

Place shells on baking sheet and bake till golden brown. Cool on rack before removing the foil. They're now ready to be filled.

Fresh Fruit Tarts

> 2 slightly beaten egg yolks
> 2 cups milk
> 1 3-ounce package *regular* vanilla pudding mix
> 2 3-ounce packages cream cheese
> 2 egg whites
> ¼ cup sugar
> 8 baked tart shells, 3½ inches in diameter, cooled
> Fresh fruits

Combine beaten egg yolks and milk. Cook pudding mix according to package directions, *using the egg-milk mixture as the liquid.* Remove from heat. Cut cream cheese in pieces and add to hot pudding. Beat till cheese is melted. Let mixture cool about 10 minutes.

Beat egg whites to soft peaks. Gradually add sugar, beating till stiff peaks form. Fold egg whites into pudding. Spoon into tart shells. Chill. Just before serving, spoon sugared fresh strawberries, blueberries, or peach halves over tarts. Makes 8 servings.

Strawberry-Cheese Tarts

> Graham Cracker Tart Shells
> ¼ cup sugar
> 2 cups sliced, fresh strawberries
> 1½ teaspoons unflavored gelatin
> 1 3-ounce package cream cheese
> ¼ cup sugar
> 1 6-ounce can evaporated milk, chilled icy cold
> 2 tablespoons lemon juice

Graham Cracker Tart Shells: Combine 1¼ cups fine graham cracker crumbs, ¼ cup sugar, and 6 tablespoons melted butter or margarine; mix. Press firmly into eight 3½-inch tart pans; chill the tart shells thoroughly.

Sprinkle ¼ cup sugar over sliced strawberries; let stand. Drain, reserving ¼ cup syrup. Soften gelatin in reserved syrup. Dissolve gelatin over hot water. Beat cream cheese with ¼ cup sugar till fluffy. Add gelatin.

In chilled bowl, whip icy cold evaporated milk till fluffy. Add lemon juice and beat to stiff peaks. Fold in cheese mixture, then fold in strawberries. Spoon into chilled tart shells. Chill till firm, about 2 hours. Serves 8.

Ham Newburg Tarts

    Cheese Tart Shells
  2 **tablespoons chopped green pepper**
  6 **tablespoons butter or margarine**
  3 **tablespoons all-purpose flour**
1½ **cups light cream**
  3 **tablespoons dry white wine**
  3 **beaten egg yolks**
  2 **cups cubed fully cooked ham**
  1 **3-ounce can sliced mushrooms,**
      drained

Cheese Tart Shells: Sift together 1 cup sifted all-purpose flour and ¼ teaspoon salt. Cut in ⅓ cup shortening till pieces are the size of small peas. Stir in 2 ounces process Swiss cheese, shredded (½ cup). Sprinkle about 4 tablespoons cold water, a tablespoon at a time, over mixture, tossing gently with fork. Repeat till all is moistened. Form into a ball. Roll ⅛ inch thick. Cut in four 6-inch circles. Fit into tart pans, crimping edges high. Prick bottom and sides. Bake at 450° till golden, 12 to 14 minutes. Remove from pans.

    Meanwhile, in medium saucepan cook green pepper in butter till tender. Blend in flour. Add cream all at once. Cook and stir till thickened and bubbly. Blend in wine; heat through. Stir some of the hot mixture into egg yolks; return to saucepan. Add ham and mushrooms. Cook and stir over low heat just till mixture begins to bubble. Spoon the mixture into warm tart shells. Makes 4 servings.

TARTAR SAUCE—A mayonnaise-based sauce containing chopped vegetables, such as pickles, onions, and parsley. Good with seafood, it can be made at home or purchased. (See also *Sauce.*)

Tartar Sauce

  1 **cup mayonnaise or salad dressing**
  3 **tablespoons finely chopped dill**
      pickle
  1 **tablespoon snipped parsley**
  2 **teaspoons chopped, canned**
      pimiento
  1 **teaspoon grated onion**

Combine all ingredients. Chill. Makes 1 cup.

TARTRATE BAKING POWDER—A leavening agent that is composed of baking soda, cream of tartar, tartaric acid, and cornstarch or flour. It is a single-action baking powder, and reacts very quickly when introduced to liquid, even at room temperature. When combined with liquid in mixture for baked products, carbon dioxide is given off, causing the dough to rise. (See also *Baking Powder.*)

TASTE—1. The physical sense that enables a person to perceive the flavor of food or beverage by means of special cells, the taste buds, located mainly on the tongue. 2. Sampling a small amount of food. Food-tasting, is also a highly developed technique requiring specialized training.

    The four basic tastes of food—sweet, sour, salty, and bitter—are sensed on different areas of the tongue. Sweet-sensitive taste buds are mostly at the tip, bitter at the base, sour along the sides, and salt on the sides and tip.

    The aroma of food also has a bearing on taste. It is this combination of taste and smell that determines what you think of a food, plus your judgment of how that food should taste.

    To taste food effectively, here are a few professional pointers to follow: taste hot foods really heated and cold foods cold; take a small sample, but make sure that it touches all areas of your tongue; and don't forget to sniff foods to see if any one flavoring ingredient stands out too much or if the total effect rouses your appetite properly.

TAUTOG (*tô tog,' -tôg'*)—A saltwater game fish, also called blackfish, that is found along the shorelines of the North American Atlantic coast. The fish averages between two and three pounds. The meat from the tautog is juicy and white with a very mild flavor. Prepare this fish by either baking, broiling, or panfrying.

TAWNY PORT—A port wine, usually blended, with a characteristic brown-tinged, red color and soft, delicate flavor. The tawny port produced both in Portugal and in the United States gets its color by aging in oak casks. (See also *Port.*)

TEA *(beverage)*—A beverage made from leaves of the tea plant. The plant is an evergreen shrub or small tree with white blossoms belonging to the camellia family. The botanical name is *thea*. Tea flourishes in the warm, humid, tropical and subtropical regions and also is grown at higher altitudes. In fact, some of the best tea grows at altitudes of 6,000 feet.

Both the people of China and those of India have legends on tea drinking, some describing its origins as early as 2737 B.C. But whenever tea drinking began, it seems certain that the beverage we enjoy today originally was used primarily as a medicine for treatment of various ills.

The word tea was first spelled in this way in 1660; however, it was pronounced *tay* until the mid-eighteenth century when the familiar, present-day pronunciation became popular. Actually, the word is derived from Chinese words *chah* (Cantonese) or *tay* (Amoy). While many countries followed the Cantonese word, the Dutch picked up the word *tay* and over the years corrupted it to *thee*, and eventually to the present-day English word, tea. The English also have nicknamed tea, Rosey Lee.

Tea has had a colorful history. It was first introduced to Japan from China in the late sixth century, but another seven centuries passed before tea became popular. From Japan, tea was introduced into Java and other lands of the Far East.

The Dutch were the first to bring tea back to Europe in the 1600s, where it became the national beverage years later. At first, it was an expensive commodity enjoyed only by the gentry, but later it became popular with all of the classes. It even became a fashionable ladies' beverage in the 1600s as a result of the marriage of the Portuguese princess, Catherine of Braganza, a fancier of tea, to Charles II. She became England's first queen to drink the beverage.

Although tea did not appear in the American colonies until the mid-seventeenth century, it played an important part in the formation of the United States. In order to maintain the British-held monopoly on tea shipped to the colonies by the East India Company, the British levied a tax on all tea purchased by the colonists. This tax led to the famous Boston Tea Party, which, in turn, helped to bring about the American Revolution.

Actually, it's a wonder the colonists ever tried tea for a second time, for the tea they drank was nothing like the fragrant beverage people enjoy today. The colonists first boiled the leaves for a long time then drank this bitter beverage without milk or sugar. Then they sprinkled salt on the 'tired' leaves and ate them with butter. In addition to those drawbacks, the cost of tea was frightening—ranging from $30 to $50 per pound.

While the Boston Tea Party did much to diminish the American habit of tea drinking, this beverage, over the years, has been gaining steadily in popularity.

Nutritional value: Tea adds few calories to the diet. When prepared without sugar or milk, one cup of tea has only two calories, making it a good beverage for those counting calories. Tea also contains some caffeine, a mild stimulant that gives a refreshing lift. It's also a good beverage to quench the thirst and is delicious served either hot or ice-cold.

How tea is grown: Seeds from mature plants are most generally started out in nurseries and then are transplanted to their permanent garden sites. If left to grow, the bush can reach 30 feet.

Many of the young plants are pruned back and kept between three and five feet tall, causing more side branches to grow off the main stem and making harvesting easier for those who pick the leaves. The pruned trees force the flushes (sprouting new leaves) to come earlier, thus extending the picking season. At the proper times, the trees are picked, either by hand or shears. This is called plucking.

The best tea is made from the leaf bud and the next two leaves. The next leaves give tea of lesser quality. Native women pick the leaves and put them into bags or bamboo baskets ready for the factory where processing takes place.

Countries that are producers of tea include India, Ceylon, China, Japan, and Indonesia. Other producing countries include Pakistan, Formosa, U.S.S.R., and the African nations of Kenya, Malawi, Uganda, Tanzania, and Mozambique. Smaller quantities are produced in Argentina and Brazil.

The largest percentage of the tea used in America comes from India, Ceylon, and the nations of East Africa.

Types of tea: As a result of different processes, there are three basic types of tea, all from the leaves of the same kind of tea plant. The types include black tea, which gives the brewed tea a rich, hearty flavor and coppery color. This type of tea accounts for almost all of the tea consumed in the United States. Green tea is another type of tea. This type makes a light-colored brew. Oolong tea, on the other hand, is a compromise between the two types of tea—black and green—and also makes a light-colored brew.

There are thousands of varieties of tea, often named for where they grow, such as Darjeeling, Assam, Formosa, and Java.

Much of the tea on the market is packaged as a blend of a number of varieties. The blends are determined by tea experts to give just the right brew desired. Tea is chosen for color, body, bouquet, and flavor. As a result, you can generally choose the blend that you like best. Some blends also have added flavors from flowers, fruit peels, and spices.

How tea is processed: For black and oolong tea, the freshly picked leaves are first withered by exposing them to the

Serve tall, cooling glasses of Iced Tea plain or with a bit of lemon juice and/or sugar. If the tea becomes cloudy before serving, add a little boiling water to make it sparkle.

sun or by forcing heated air over racks of leaves. This makes the leaves soft and pliable and takes from 12 to 24 hours.

The next step is rolling, which breaks the leaf cells and frees the juices. The twisted pieces that come from the rolling machine are then broken up by coarse mesh sieves or roll-breakers. The fine leaves are ready for fermentation, while the coarser leaves are rolled again.

Fermentation (oxidation) is the next step used when making black and oolong tea. The leaves are spread out in a cool, humid room where they absorb oxygen and change color—to a bright copper. This reduces the astringency of the tea and takes between 20 and 60 minutes. The leaves are partially fermented for oolong, resulting in a greenish brown leaf coloring. Then, the leaves are dried or fired, which stops fermentation.

On the other hand, the leaves for making green tea are not withered as for black and oolong, but rather are steamed and heated to soften the leaves. After steaming, the leaves are rolled and dried. Unlike black tea, the leaves for green tea retain their green color.

Grades of tea: The next step after drying is grading the tea into leaf size. This is done in sieves with graduated mesh that divide tea into leaf and broken grades.

The leaf grades include Orange Pekoe (pronounced peck-o), Pekoe, and Pekoe Souchong. Tea made from these grades is more popular in Europe.

Broken grades of tea include Broken Orange Pekoe, Broken Pekoe, Broken Pekoe Souchong, Fannings, and Dust. They make up the largest percentage of crop and produce a stronger tea.

Packaging tea: All the tea that you find on the American supermarket shelf has been passed by the United States Tea Examiner before it is sent to the tea companies for blending and packaging as loose tea or in tea bags, or before it is prepared for instant or iced-tea mixtures.

When you consider that tea was discovered thousands of years ago, it is surprising to learn that the widespread American habit of using tea bags is a recent innovation. Until 1904, tea was packaged loose in cans or boxes. However, tea bags happened quite accidentally one day when a tea merchant sent out some samples of his tea in small, silk bags, rather than in the customary tins. Rather than emptying the tea into a pot and using it as loose tea, people brewed the tea samples using the small packets. Over the years, tea packed in bags became popular. Today, tea is prepared in bags made of special filter paper.

Instant tea is a more recent invention. During the 1950s, the industry developed a powdered tea by using a concentrated brew and then removing the water by means of a drying process. From the instant tea came the mixes, combinations of instant tea, sugar, and flavorings. Canned ice tea is also available.

How to select: Personal preference determines whether you choose black, green, or oolong tea and whether it is loose packed, packaged in tea bags, or processed as instant tea. Popular black tea varieties include Assam, Ceylon, Darjeeling, Earl Grey, English Breakfast, Keemun, and Lapsang Souchong. Popular green teas include Basket Fired and Gunpowder. The most popular oolong and mixed teas are Formosa Oolong and Jasmine, scented with jasmine blossoms. Experiment with different varieties.

How to store: Keep loose tea or tea bags in a tightly covered container. Use the tea within six months for best flavor.

How to use: Tea makes delightful hot and cold beverages and punches that are real thirst-quenchers. Hot tea is served most often with milk rather than with cream, or with lemon and sugar.

Iced tea is also a popular favorite and is most often presented with sugar and lemon. It is an invention of the twentieth century and was first introduced to the public at the St. Louis World's Fair in 1904. Because of the hot weather, fairgoers were not very enthusiastic about sampling the hot tea being promoted at the Far East Pavilion. So, an inventive young Englishman from India decided to

---

How to make tea

Use black tea, green tea, oolong, and mixed teas interchangeably whenever you prepare hot tea or iced tea beverages.

Hot tea: Place 1 teaspoon loose tea or 1 tea bag for each cup desired in a teapot that has been heated by rinsing with boiling water. Bring freshly drawn cold water to a full, rolling boil. Immediately pour over tea. Steep tea about 5 minutes. For tea of uniform strength, stir briskly and serve at once. If you want weaker tea, dilute by adding a little hot water.

Iced tea: Heat 1 quart freshly drawn cold water to full rolling boil; remove from heat. Add 8 to 12 tea bags or 3 tablespoons loose tea at once. Let steep, uncovered, 5 minutes. Remove tea bags or strain out loose tea. Add 1 quart freshly drawn cold water. Serve over ice cubes in tall glasses.

Keep the tea at room temperature because refrigeration may cause cloudiness. If tea does cloud, you can restore its clear color by adding a little boiling water.

Instant tea: Prepare hot or iced tea quickly by using instant tea or the iced tea mixes. Follow the speedy directions on the label.

---

pour the hot tea over ice. People loved it and found it delightfully refreshing. From that time on, iced tea has been one of the favorite summertime drinks in the United States. (See *Beverage, Tea* [*occasion*] for additional information.)

Pineapple Frostea

    2 tablespoons instant tea powder
    3 cups ice water
    6 tablespoons frozen pineapple
        concentrate, thawed
    1 pint pineapple sherbet

Dissolve tea in water; add pineapple concentrate. Pour into 6 glasses. Add a scoop of sherbet to each. Stir slightly to muddle. Serves 6.

Spiced Tea

Hot tea with a spicy, fruit flavor—

    6 cups water
    1 teaspoon whole cloves
    1 inch stick cinnamon
    2½ tablespoons loose tea
    ¾ cup orange juice
    2 tablespoons lemon juice
    ½ cup sugar

Combine water, whole cloves, and stick cinnamon in a saucepan. Heat to boiling. Add tea. Cover and steep 5 minutes; strain.

Heat orange juice, lemon juice, and sugar to boiling. Stir and add to the hot tea. Serve piping hot. Makes 6 to 8 servings.

Iced Fruit Tea

    3 cups boiling water
    2 tablespoons loose tea *or* 6
        tea bags
    ½ cup sugar
        • • •
    ½ cup orange juice
    ⅓ cup lemon juice
    2 7-ounce bottles ginger ale,
        chilled (about 2 cups)

Pour boiling water over tea; cover and steep 5 minutes; strain. Add sugar and stir till dissolved. Add fruit juices. Pour into pitcher half full of ice. Just before serving, carefully pour ginger ale down side of pitcher. Trim with mint, if desired. Makes 5½ cups.

Amber Tea Delight

Apricot nectar adds a special flavor—

    4 cups hot tea
    2 12-ounce cans apricot nectar
    2 cups orange juice
    ½ cup sugar
    ½ cup lemon juice
    1 28-ounce bottle ginger ale

Combine tea, nectar, orange juice, sugar, and lemon juice. Chill. Before serving, add ginger ale. Pour over ice cubes to serve. Serves 24.

TEA *(occasion)*—An afternoon party where any number of people gather together for a light snack and beverage. Of course, tea is always served, but other beverages have also become accepted at this traditionally feminine form of entertaining.

An English hostess, the Duchess of Bedford, is credited with introducing this delightful occasion. She chose to fill in the long gap between an early lunch and the late court dinner by serving her lady friends a cup of tea and a bite to eat to accompany the late-afternoon gossip. The idea soon spread to include several tea breaks during the day.

Much is made of the Englishman's tea-drinking habits. Not only do they drink tea with their meals, but they take an afternoon tea break, similar to the American coffee break. The English also serve what is called a high tea or meat tea. This type of tea is more of a meal and is usually served in the evening when dinner or the main meal is eaten at noon, often the case with weekend dining. Accompanying the tea will be meats or fish, cooked dishes, and possibly tiny cakes. The English high tea can be likened to the American supper (see *English Cookery*).

The afternoon tea that American women frequently find themselves involved with, either as hostess or guest, takes the form of either a semiformal or informal occasion. The time for a tea is socially prescribed—between 3:00 and 6:00 in the afternoon. It is, strictly speaking, a social occasion. A tea is an easy way to entertain guests without the work and expense of a sit-down dinner and the perfect time to introduce a new neighbor or honor an out-of-town guest.

The number of people invited to a tea is flexible, and you can invite people of all age groups. When you want to entertain a large number of guests, a tea is a good solution to accomplish this task. Since

Invite a few neighbors over for a refreshing cup of tea. Make an occasion out of the gathering, and serve the tea in your fanciest china cups. Bring out your silver teapot and accessories.

the guests are mobile during the larger, semiformal tea, you don't have to provide much seating or table space. In addition, food preparation is kept to a minimum, since the star of the food at the party is generally the beverage and since small amounts of food are usually consumed.

One of the most essential foods of the party is the tea itself. It must be brewed and served properly. In warm weather you might want to offer iced tea as a cooling refreshment in place of hot tea, especially if it is an informal occasion. The food is the other essential ingredient. With delicately flavored tea, plan to serve plainer types of foods, such as buttered breads or a pound cake. Coffee, chocolate, or punch, on the other hand, which frequently appear on the tea table, go well with more highly flavored foods because these beverages have stronger flavors than does tea. If you plan to serve another beverage in addition to tea, prepare foods that go well with both beverages.

When planning a menu for the tea party, keep in mind that the foods should vary in texture, flavor, color, and ingredients. Another main consideration is to choose foods that are not messy to eat, such as cake with a sticky frosting.

Sweets include soft cakes and cookies, crisp meringues, and creamy mints. Not so sweet foods include crunchy nuts, miniature cream puffs filled with a seasoned meat or fish salad, fruit and nut breads, and dainty sandwiches. Use a variety of breads for the sandwiches to add color contrast, and avoid repeating flavors. For example, if the cookies have almonds in them, avoid using almonds in the nut bread or in the sandwich spread.

When you have decided that you want to give a tea party, consider the number of guests that you'll want. If you want to invite a few close friends, chances are it will be an informal, intimate get-together. However, if your guest list keeps growing and you decide to invite a large group, why not plan a more formal occasion?

Small, informal teas: Invitations to the informal gathering are generally handled personally or by telephone. The tea can be as simple as tea for two, or more people can be invited. Make it a party even if you and your neighbor are having a cup of tea together. Serve the tea in dainty cups and offer something with it to eat. It takes only a minute or two while the kettle boils to make a cup of tea into a little occasion. Choose a pleasant spot in your home where you'll want to serve tea, such as the porch or patio when the weather is warm, or in front of the fireplace during the cold winter months.

For entertaining a few more friends, set up a large tray with all the necessary items—teapot, cups, milk and sugar, a plate with lemon slices, plates and napkins, and any flatware that will be needed for the food and beverage.

Usually, the food is very simple and can be limited to one of the following: cookies, small sandwiches, buttered nut breads, hot rolls, tarts, tiny cakes, or pastries. If you choose cookies, it's nice to offer a choice of at least two kinds. Remember that tea is just a between-meal snack, so serve dainty foods, prettily arranged.

At the informal gathering, the tea tray can be placed on the coffee table or other low serving table. Or be a bit more elegant and use a tea cart or set up a small table and cover it with a dainty cloth. The hostess always pours at the informal type of tea. The guests, however, pick up their own food, napkins, and flatware.

Then, sit back and watch the atmosphere glow as good conversation takes place over the friendly teapot.

Large, semiformal teas: Preparations for this type of tea take a bit more time than for the smaller gathering. You'll need a large table and room enough around the table for people to move freely. The tea table should be covered with your prettiest cloth. A centerpiece of flowers or a centerpiece carrying out a theme is also in order. Candles may be used, especially if the sun is not shining brightly. If candles are on the table, they should be lit. Gleaming silver and exquisite china also add to a beautifully set table. Since serving is usually handled buffet-style, it is important that the table be especially attractive because everyone will have a chance to scrutinize it closely.

You have a choice of setting up your serving table with food on both sides and the beverage service at both ends. Or set the table for serving on only one side with the beverage at one end.

The two-sided service works best for a large crowd. Make the food on both sides of the table exact duplicates. The only difference is that cream and sugar accompany the coffee service, while lemon, milk, and sugar are at the opposite end with the tea service. Then, guests preferring coffee or punch take one side and tea fans take the other.

Before the day of the tea, ask a close friend or two to pour. If the party is going to last several hours, you might ask additional friends to relieve those who are pouring. This way, you will be free to make guests feel at home and you will be able to replenish the beverages and trays of food as the need arises.

The one who is pouring the beverage hands the filled cup to guests. There are two schools of thought on when the beverage should be served. Some say it's picked up first, others say it should be the last item. Guests help themselves to plate, napkin, flatware, and food.

The plate should be large enough to accommodate the cup and saucer plus snack. Or use smaller plates that hold cup plus food. Plates are important! If

For a small, informal tea, set up a tea tray for easy serving. The tea tray holds tea, hot water, cream (milk), sugar, and lemon slices (with tiny fork). Stack folded napkins between plates and place cups on saucers at back or side of tray within easy reach. Or place nearby on table. If smaller plates are used, omit the saucers. Also arrange flatware on tray. Place food on table next to tea tray. Hostess pours tea and adds water, milk, sugar, and lemon at guests' request.

Set up a table for a larger, semiformal tea with beverage at one end and food along one side. Place centerpiece along edge nearest wall. Or set the tea table for two-way travel. Place coffee and accompaniments or punch on tray at one end, tea with its accompaniments on tray at other end, and decorations in center. Set cups and saucers to left of pourer. Guests pick up flatware, plate, napkin, food, and then are handed the beverage, which has cream or sugar added, if desired.

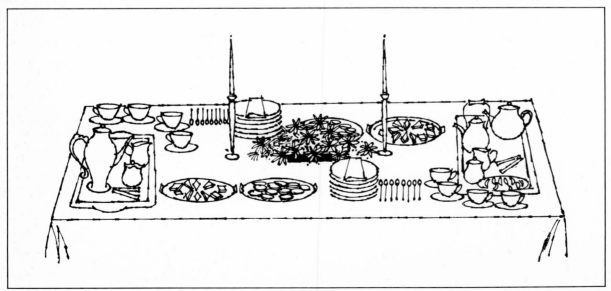

you have ever had food and napkin in one hand and a beverage in the other, wondering how you were going to manage both, you can appreciate plates.

The following recipes are just a few of the possibilities to choose from when planning a tea. (See *Beverage, Bread, Cookie, Sandwich, Tea [beverage]* for additional recipes and information.)

Starlight Cakes

　　¾ cup shortening
　1½ cups sugar
　1½ teaspoons vanilla
　2¼ cups sifted cake flour
　　3 teaspoons baking powder
　　1 cup milk
　　5 stiff-beaten egg whites
　　　Confectioners' Icing
　　　Silver decorator candies

In large mixer bowl cream shortening and sugar. Add vanilla. Sift together flour, baking powder, and 1 teaspoon salt. Add to creamed mixture alternately with milk, beating after each addition. Beat 2 minutes at medium speed of electric mixer. Fold in egg whites.

Pour into well-greased and floured star-shaped molds (individual gelatin molds), using ¼ cup batter for each. Bake at 375° for 20 to 25 minutes. Cool 5 minutes before removing from pans. Place cakes on rack over baking sheet; spoon Confectioners' Icing evenly over cakes. Decorate with silver candies. Makes 20.

Confectioners' Icing: In bowl stir together 6 cups sifted confectioners' sugar and ⅓ to ½ cup milk till of pouring consistency. Add 1 teaspoon vanilla and ⅛ teaspoon salt.

Bite-Sized Chicken Puffs

　　2 cups finely chopped, cooked
　　　　chicken
　　¼ cup finely chopped celery
　　2 tablespoons dry white wine
　　2 tablespoons chopped, canned
　　　　pimiento
　　⅓ cup mayonnaise
　　⅔ cup water
　　1 stick piecrust mix, crumbled
　　2 eggs

Combine first 5 ingredients, ¼ teaspoon salt, and dash pepper; chill the mixture.

In small saucepan heat water to boiling. Add crumbled piecrust mix; stir vigorously over low heat till pastry forms a ball and leaves sides of pan. Cook 1 minute more, stirring constantly. Add eggs and beat on low speed of electric mixer for 2 minutes. Drop dough from rounded teaspoon onto *ungreased* baking sheet. Bake at 425° till puffed, golden brown, and dry, about 20 to 25 minutes. Transfer puffs to rack; cool slowly away from draft. Split and fill with chicken mixture. Makes 42.

Arrange a tray of Starlight Cakes on the tea table. For other seasons of the year, vary the shape of the cakes with different molds.

TEAKETTLE—A metal kettle with a spout and handle that is used for boiling water. Despite its name, a teakettle is not used for brewing or serving tea; however, the water used in the preparation of tea may be heated in a teakettle.

The teakettle may be a plain metal container or a trimmed, colorful, enamel-coated kettle that is frequently found as a decorative item in the kitchen. Some teakettles have a whistle in the spout. As the water boils, the pressure from the escaping steam causes the whistle to blow, informing the homemaker that the water is boiling and ready for use.

TEAL *(tēl)*—A freshwater wild duck that usually is prepared by roasting. (See also *Duck and Duckling.*)

TEAPOT—A decorative china, pottery, ceramic, or glass container with cover, spout, and handle, used for brewing and serving tea. After the tea is brewed in the china pot, it may be served from that pot or transferred to a silver teapot.

TEMPLE ORANGE—A sweet, rich-flavored, juicy orange of the mandarin type. It has a deep, orange color and an oval shape. Frequently, the skin is pebbly. The variety is named after William Chase Temple, once a prominent leader in the Florida citrus business.

Although there has been widespread speculation as to its origin, the exact parentage of Temple oranges is not known. The fruits have the shape, easy peeling, and easy segmenting characteristics of mandarin oranges such as tangerines. Their sweet, juicy flavor suggests a relationship to sweet oranges, yet the disease resistance follows sour oranges more closely. In any event, most authorities agree that the eating qualities of Temple oranges make them one of the outstanding citrus fruits in America.

Temple oranges first grew in Winter Park, Florida. They have remained mainly Florida-produced fruits, as their cultivation has been less successful in other areas. These oranges are in season from January-March. (See *Mandarin Orange*, *Orange* for additional information.)

TEMPURA *(tem' pōō rä,' tem pōōr' uh)*—A Japanese dish of seafood and/or vegetables that are batter coated and fried in deep hot fat. The small, batter-dipped pieces of food are fried till the almost-sheer crust is a light golden brown.

Some of the foods prepared by Japanese cooks are shrimp, prawns, scallops, mushrooms, green beans, green peppers, sweet potatoes, eggplant, young carrots, and sprigs of parsley. They frequently use sesame oil, rice oil, peanut oil, or soybean oil for frying. On the other hand, American recipes call for any bland cooking oil.

The pieces of food are frequently eaten as they are fried and are accompanied by a sauce flavored with soy and condiments of grated radish and fresh gingerroot.

Plan a party around Japanese tempura and cook the food at the table in front of your guests. Then, serve it while still hot. Accompany the foods with condiments and rice; then, serve fresh fruit and tea for dessert. Small cups of warm sake (rice wine) add to the authenticity of the party. (See also *Oriental Cookery.*)

Tips on tempura

● Prepare sauces and condiments ahead of time to avoid last-minute preparation. Cover and chill them till ready to use.
● Mix batter together just before using.
● Use a few ice cubes to keep the batter well chilled while it is being used. The ice keeps the batter cold without diluting it.
● A fresh, bland cooking oil is best to use for frying the batter-coated foods.
● To maintain the temperature of the oil during cooking, use a deep electric skillet that has a thermostatic control.
● To keep the oil free from extra batter, use one set of tongs to dip food into the batter, then use another set of tongs for frying the batter-coated food in the oil.
● Remove any extra drops of batter that float on surface of the fat during cooking.
● Cook only a few pieces of food at a time to avoid lowering the temperature of the oil.
● Use a rack that is set over a tray to drain the batter-coated fried foods.

Japanese Tempura

Raw shrimp, peeled and cleaned
Assorted fresh vegetables such
  as asparagus spears, parsley,
  sweet potatoes, spinach,
  mushrooms, and green beans
Salad oil
1 cup sifted all-purpose flour
1 slightly beaten egg
2 tablespoons salad oil
½ teaspoon sugar
Tempura Condiments

Wash and dry shrimp and vegetables well. Slice or cut vegetables into strips, if necessary. Fill skillet ½ full with salad oil; heat to 360° to 365°. Make batter by combining flour, 1 cup ice water, egg, 2 tablespoons salad oil, sugar, and ½ teaspoon salt; beat just till moistened. Stir in 1 or 2 ice cubes to keep batter chilled. Dip shrimp and vegetables in cold batter. Fry in hot oil till light brown; drain.

Serve with Tempura Condiments: **1.** grated fresh gingerroot; **2.** equal parts grated turnip and radish, combined; and **3.** ½ cup prepared mustard mixed with 3 tablespoons soy sauce.

TENDERIZATION—The process of softening the tough fibers of meat, making them easier to chew and more palatable. There are several ways to tenderize meat. Commercially, an enzyme is sometimes used, which makes the meat more tender as it cooks. Or, some meat pieces are scored with a machine that cuts the connective tissue, as in minute steaks. Aging and grinding also tenderize meat. At home, meat can be tenderized by pounding, by treating it with a commercial tenderizer, by cooking with moist heat, or marinating.

TENDERLOIN—The tender, long, tapering muscle of the loin section of beef, pork, and lamb. Beef tenderloin has little fat; pork tenderloin contains a small amount of fat. Lamb tenderloin, being small, is not sold separately. Tenderloin, alone, is boneless, but when attached to the loin it is the muscle of beef T-bone, porterhouse, and some sirloin steaks; pork loin chops and sirloin roasts; and lamb loin and sirloin chops and roasts.

Occasionally, a whole beef tenderloin is purchased; however, it is more frequently marketed as fillets, filets mignons, Châteaubriands, tournedos, and tenderloin tips. Tenderloin cubes are often used for beef fondue, while other cuts are broiled, panbroiled, and panfried.

To prepare tenderloins roast or braise whole pork tenderloins and panfry, braise, or broil slices of tenderloin.

Tenderloin with Orange Sauce

Brown one 2-pound pork tenderloin in 2 tablespoons butter; remove meat. In same skillet cook ½ cup chopped onion till tender. Add 1 teaspoon grated orange peel, ⅔ cup orange juice, ⅓ cup dry sherry, 2 tablespoons sugar, 2 teaspoons salt, dash pepper, and 1 medium bay leaf. Return meat; cover. Simmer till tender, 1 hour; turn occasionally. Remove meat. Combine 1 tablespoon *each* cornstarch and cold water; stir into orange mixture. Bring to boiling; cook and stir 1 to 2 minutes. Drizzle some sauce over meat. Serves 6 to 8.

Spoon some of the wine-flavored sauce over slices of Tenderloin with Orange Sauce, then pass remaining sauce with the meat.

Roast Pork Tenderloin

2 slices bacon
1 1-pound pork tenderloin
⅓ cup chopped onion
1 tablespoon butter or margarine
1 8-ounce can tomato sauce
3 tablespoons chopped sweet pickle
2 tablespoons vinegar
1 tablespoon snipped parsley
1 teaspoon sugar

Arrange bacon over top of pork tenderloin. Place roast on rack in shallow roasting pan, tucking thin end of meat under. Roast, uncovered, at 350° till meat thermometer registers 170°, about 35 to 45 minutes.

Cook onion in butter till tender but not brown. Add tomato sauce, sweet pickle, vinegar, parsley, and sugar. Simmer sauce, uncovered, for 10 minutes. Serve sauce with roast tenderloin. Makes 4 or 5 servings.

Broiled Beef Fillets

½ cup claret
2 tablespoons soy sauce
½ cup finely chopped onion
2 tablespoons finely snipped
parsley
1 clove garlic, minced
Dash pepper
4 4-ounce beef tenderloin fillets,
1 inch thick

Combine first 6 ingredients. Place fillets in plastic bag; pour marinade over. Close bag. Marinate 2 hours in refrigerator; press bag occasionally to distribute marinade. Remove fillets from bag; reserve marinade. Broil steaks 3 inches from heat 7 minutes. Turn; broil 6 minutes longer or to desired doneness.

Heat reserved marinade to boiling; spoon over broiled fillets. Makes 4 servings.

TENNESSEE HAM—A country-style ham produced in Tennessee. These hams are heavily cured and smoked. (See also *Ham*.)

TEPID—A word that is used to describe the lukewarm or moderately warm temperature of water and other liquids.

TEQUILA (*tuh kē′ luh*)—A Mexican alcoholic beverage, usually colorless, that is distilled from the pineapplelike heart of the agave plant, a type of cactus. The potent liquid is named after Tequila, Mexico, where the beverage has been made for over two centuries. When it is produced in other parts of Mexico, the beverage must be called mescal.

Although tequila is most often used in the Margarita cocktail in the United States, Mexicans prefer to consume this powerful beverage straight. Traditionally, a shot of tequila is held in one hand with salt on the back or thumbnail of the other hand and a lime wedge secured between thumb and forefinger. The sequence in which these three foods are taken varies —some people first suck on the lime followed by ingesting some salt and downing the tequila; others take some salt, then tequila, and finally lime juice. Tequila drinking in either of these fashions is much enjoyed by Mexicans for a quenching refreshment.

Tequila is made by normal extraction and distillation procedures. The mature agave bases are cut from the plants, then are cut open. The sweet syrup inside called *aguamiel* is allowed to run off as the bases are steamed in ovens for about eight hours. Subsequently, the bases are pulverized and the remaining sap is pressed out. Fermentation of the sap takes place in large vats for several days. Pot stills then perform the distillation process. Most tequilas are not aged. (See also *Wines and Spirits*.)

TERIYAKI (*ter ē yä′ kē*)—A Japanese cooking technique in which meat is marinated in a soy sauce mixture and then broiled. Fish, shellfish, beef, and chicken are commonly used in teriyaki. The marinade usually consists of sake (or sherry), ginger, and other spices along with the soy sauce. This marinade gives a delicate, sweet flavor to the meat.

Broil teriyaki in an oven, on a grill, or on a hibachi. When you are broiling, it's always a good practice to string the meat on skewers. Use the marinade as a basting sauce during the broiling or later as a glaze. (See also *Oriental Cookery*.)

Teriyaki Scallops

  1 pound frozen scallops, thawed
 ½ cup soy sauce
 ¼ cup dry sherry
  2 tablespoons sugar
  2 tablespoons salad oil
 ¾ teaspoon ground ginger
  1 clove garlic, crushed

Rinse and cut large scallops in half. Combine remaining ingredients; pour over scallops in shallow dish. Marinate 30 minutes at room temperature. Drain scallops, reserving marinade. Thread scallops on 4 skewers. Place on greased, shallow baking pan. Bake at 450° for 15 minutes, turning and basting several times with marinade. Makes 4 servings.

Teriyaki

Combine ½ cup soy sauce, ¼ cup salad oil, 2 tablespoons molasses, 2 teaspoons ground ginger, 2 teaspoons dry mustard, and 6 cloves garlic, minced. Mix well. Using 1½ pounds chuck *or* round steak (1 inch thick), slice into strips ¼ inch thick. Use instant unseasoned meat tenderizer on steak according to label directions. Add meat to marinade, stirring to coat, and let stand 15 minutes at room temperature. Lace meat strips accordion-fashion on skewers. Broil over *hot* coals, to desired doneness, about 5 to 7 minutes. Turn frequently; baste with marinade. Serves 6.

TERRAPIN *(ter' uh pin)*—An edible turtle that lives in fresh and brackish waters in North America. They are used in making soups and stews. (See also *Turtle.*)

TERRINE *(tuh rēn')*—1. A casserole dish made of pottery. 2. A meat, fish, or game mixture similar to pâté, which is baked in a terrine dish and served cold. Terrine resembles a meat pie without a crust.

TETRAZZINI *(te' truh zē' nē)*—A dish consisting of chicken or turkey, pasta, and a rich cream sauce. Mushrooms, slivered almonds, sherry, nutmeg, and cheese are added for flavor. This dish was named for the opera singer, Luisa Tetrazzini.

Turkey Tetrazzini

  6 ounces spaghetti, broken up
 ¼ cup butter or margarine
 ½ cup all-purpose flour
2¾ cups chicken broth
  1 cup light cream
 ¼ cup dry sherry
  1 teaspoon salt
    Dash pepper
  1 6-ounce can sliced mushrooms, drained
 ¼ cup chopped green pepper
  2 cups diced, cooked turkey *or* chicken
 ½ cup shredded Parmesan cheese

Cook spaghetti in boiling, salted water till just tender (do not overcook); drain. Melt butter; blend in flour. Stir broth into flour mixture. Add cream. Cook and stir till mixture is thickened and bubbly. Add wine, salt, pepper, drained spaghetti, mushrooms, green pepper, and cooked turkey *or* chicken. Turn into an 11¾x7½x1¾-inch baking dish. Sprinkle top with Parmesan cheese. Bake at 350° about 30 minutes. Makes 5 or 6 servings.

THANKSGIVING—A national holiday in the United States for giving thanks for the year's blessings. It is held in November on a date set by Congress.

From the earliest times, man has set aside days of thanksgiving. However, the holiday that we celebrate today is distinctively American. It stems from the Pilgrims' celebration of the first bountiful harvest in Plymouth during the autumn of 1621. Governor William Bradford declared a day of thanksgiving for the bountiful harvest which they had made. Approximately 55 Pilgrims and 90 Indians were present for this occasion. They feasted on turkey, venison, duck, geese, seafoods, berries, plums, corn bread, wheat bread, hoe and ash cakes, pumpkin pie, and Indian pudding.

For many years, Thanksgiving was not a set holiday in America. Various states declared days of thanksgiving at different times during the year. It was not until 1863 that President Lincoln proclaimed one national holiday to be set aside for giving thanks. This act was largely due to the efforts of Mrs. Sarah Josepha Hale, editor of the famous *Godey's Lady's Book*.

Thanksgiving traditions: Today's celebration of Thanksgiving has many traditions that come from the first celebration of the Pilgrims. Families and friends, for instance, gather for the event just as the Pilgrims and Indians joined together in that feast. A religious overtone of thanksgiving for the year's blessings prevails during the day. Decorations carry out the theme of the fall harvest with golden pumpkins, fall leaves, polished apples, nuts, and corn. The menu also is much like the food served by the Pilgrims.

Traditionally, a roasted turkey is the main feature of the Thanksgiving Day dinner. The foods that complement the turkey vary from region to region. However, most families include cranberries, mashed potatoes or candied sweet potatoes, stuffing, hot bread, pumpkin pie, mincemeat pie, and Indian pudding.

Underlying all these traditions is the spirit of the occasion—the thankful mood for the fortunes of the past year and the joyous reunions and feasting.

Meat thermometers should extend to the center of the meat. Locate thermometers in the thickest part away from any bone or fat.

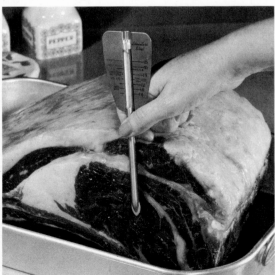

THERMOMETER—An instrument for measuring temperature. It consists of a liquid such as mercury in a slender, glass tube, or coiled bimetal strips that expand or contract with changes in temperature. The temperature is indicated by the height of the mercury or a pointer at a degree mark. There are many kinds of thermometers—candy, deep-frying, meat, oven, refrigerator, and freezer.

Because the thermometer points out the exact temperature of the food or appliance, it takes the guesswork out of cooking. However, they are useful only if you know the temperature required.

Similar in size and shape, candy and deep-frying thermometers are often interchangeable. These thermometers have a clip that fastens onto the side of the pan, so the bulb does not touch the bottom of the pan and register the pan's temperature instead of the food's temperature.

Candy thermometers are used when making candies, jellies, syrups, and frostings, for it is vital to cook these mixtures to the correct temperature.

Initially, deep-frying thermometers show when fat is hot enough to begin frying. Then, they are used to show when the heat should be adjusted during frying to keep a constant temperature—this results in crisp, evenly cooked food.

Meat thermometers differ from candy thermometers by having a sharper metal point. This end is inserted into the center of the meat, where it gets the most accurate reading. It should not touch any fat or bone. On poultry, it is inserted into the center of the inside thigh muscle.

Some ranges come with meat thermometer attachments. These thermometers are inserted like others but are also connected to the oven thermostat. The oven turns off or an alarm sounds when the meat reaches the temperature you set on the dials.

There are also thermometers made to register the temperature inside ovens, refrigerators, and freezers.

A cooking thermometer will give many years of good service if you care for it properly. Always clean it thoroughly after each use and then store it so the glass will not be broken. Check occasionally to see that it is registering properly. To test a meat, candy, or deep-frying thermometer, put in boiling water. It should register 212° (boiling point of water) at sea level. If thermometer registers above or below 212°, add or subtract degrees to make the same allowance on the recipe.

THERMOSTAT—A device in an appliance which keeps a preset temperature by adjusting the heating or cooling.

THIAMINE—A B-complex vitamin, also known as the antiberiberi or appetite vitamin. It is needed for normal appetite and digestion, for a healthy nervous system, and to help change food into energy.

Thiamine isn't stored in the body, so it must be eaten daily. Provide yourself with this essential vitamin by eating pork, liver, peas, dry beans and enriched bread, and by drinking milk.

Because thiamine is water soluble and is broken down by heat, avoid both excessive cooking water and cooking time.

THICKENING AGENT—A food substance used to make the consistency of a mixture—generally, sauces, gravies, puddings, and soups—thicker. The most common are flour, cornstarch, arrowroot, tapioca, egg yolk, and bread crumbs.

There are specific ways to add thickening agents in recipes to get a smooth product without lumps or curdling. For instance, blend flour into melted fat, add liquid, then cook mixture until it is thick. Blend cornstarch with sugar and then cold liquid before any heat is applied. And blend egg yolks with a small amount of the hot mixture, then add to the entire mixture to prevent coagulating the egg.

THIMBLEBERRY—Any blackberry or raspberry with a thimble-shaped fruit.

THOUSAND ISLAND SALAD DRESSING— A mayonnaise-base salad dressing with chili sauce, pickles, pimiento, peppers, and other seasonings added for flavor. Thousand Island salad dressing was

Ladle homemade Thousand Island, flecked with green pepper and pimiento, over crisp lettuce wedges and hard-boiled egg halves for a convenient buffet salad or family dinner salad.

created in 1910 for the opening of the Blackstone Hotel in Chicago. It is especially good served over tossed salads.

Thousand Island

    1 cup mayonnaise
    3 tablespoons chili sauce
    1 tablespoon chopped green pepper
    1 teaspoon chopped canned
        pimiento
    1 teaspoon chopped chives

Blend all ingredients thoroughly. Chill. Serve with lettuce wedges. Makes 1¼ cups.

However, Thousand Island salad dressing is not only for salads. It is also a flavorful addition to a wide variety of other foods. It makes a delicious Reuben sandwich or hamburger when spread on the bread or bun. Thousand Island is often used as an ingredient in recipes such as this Tuna-Rice Salad.

Tuna-Rice Salad

Make this salad one day and serve the next day—

    ¾ cup uncooked long-grain rice
    1 10-ounce package frozen peas
    1 9¾-ounce can tuna, drained
    1 8½-ounce can pineapple tidbits,
        drained
    ½ cup chopped celery
        •   •   •
    ½ cup Thousand Island salad
        dressing
    ½ cup dairy sour cream
    2 tablespoons finely chopped green
        onion
        Lettuce cups

Cook rice according to package directions; drain. Cook peas according to package directions; drain. In bowl combine rice, peas, tuna, pineapple, and celery. Mix together the Thousand Island salad dressing, sour cream, and chopped onion; pour over rice mixture and toss lightly. Cover and chill thoroughly. Serve in lettuce cups. Makes 6 servings.

THYME *(tīm)*—An herb that is related to the mint family. There are many different varieties of thyme, but the ones used in cooking usually come from shrubby plants and have tiny, narrow, grayish green leaves. These have a slightly pungent aroma and flavor. Another variety differs from these in that it has a lemon fragrance. This is known as lemon thyme.

Thyme is native to Asia Minor and the Mediterranean area. In ancient days, the people in these regions, such as the Romans and Greeks, used thyme in many ways. They used thyme to flavor food and for medicinal purposes, grew it in gardens for the lovely lavender flowers and fragrance, bathed in thyme and water to gain courage, and spread it over floors to add fragrance and to prevent mildew.

Today, we still use thyme for many of these purposes. For example, thyme is the flavor in many commercial gargles, coughdrops, dentifrices, and mouthwashes. It is also used in many anti-mildew preparations sold in stores. Thyme is a popular garden herb today. It is grown in many areas of the United States for its beauty and for use in cooking.

Ground thyme and dried thyme leaves are available in supermarkets if you do not choose to grow your own herb. Most of this comes from France, Spain, Portugal, Greece, and California.

Uses of thyme: Thyme gives a pleasant flavor to many dishes. It goes well with fish, chicken, lamb, seafood, liver, soup, dressing, and vegetables, such as tomato, Brussels sprouts, carrots, green beans, mushrooms, and potatoes.

Thyme is a natural partner with other herbs, too. Combinations of thyme and basil are delicious, especially with tomato mixtures. Thyme also teams well with bay leaf. This pair is frequently used in French dishes. Thyme and oregano blend well in a number of dishes, too.

When seasoning with thyme, use a small amount and increase the amount to your taste as with other herbs. Usually, for each four servings you can use these guides: ⅛ to 1 teaspoon of dried leaves; ⅛ to ½ teaspoon ground thyme; and 1 to 2 teaspoons fresh leaves. (See also *Herb*.)

Red Hots on Kabob

½ pound frankfurters
⅓ cup soy sauce
⅓ cup catsup
¼ cup salad oil
2 tablespoons vinegar
1 teaspoon dried thyme leaves, crushed
1 teaspoon prepared mustard
16 small, canned onions
16 canned pineapple chunks
1 green pepper, cut in 1-inch squares
8 slices bacon

With sharp knife cut frankfurters in 1-inch pieces and score cut ends of pieces. Combine soy sauce, catsup, salad oil, vinegar, thyme, and mustard. Pour over franks, onions, pineapple, and green pepper. Chill 3 hours.

Cut bacon in half crosswise; partially cook. Wrap bacon piece around each pineapple chunk. On 9- or 10-inch skewers, alternate the chunks of franks, vegetables, and pineapple. Broil 3 to 4 inches from heat for about 12 minutes, making a quarter turn every 3 minutes. Brush with glaze each turn. Serves 4 or 5.

Meat and Macaroni Supper

½ cup chopped onion
2 tablespoons butter or margarine
1 10½-ounce can condensed cream of celery soup
1 8-ounce can tomatoes, cut up
¼ teaspoon dried thyme leaves, crushed
Dash pepper
½ 7-ounce package elbow macaroni (1 cup), cooked and drained
1 12-ounce can luncheon meat, cut in 1x½-inch strips
¼ cup chopped green pepper
¼ cup shredded process American cheese

In skillet cook onion in butter till tender but not brown. Stir in soup, tomatoes, thyme, and pepper. Add macaroni, meat, and green pepper. Spoon into 1½ quart casserole. Top with cheese. Bake, uncovered, at 350° till heated through, 35 to 40 minutes. Serves 4 to 6.

TIDBIT—A small or choice piece of food. This word often is used to describe small, spicy or sweet portions of food. For this reason, some packaged foods are labeled tidbit. Pineapple tidbits, for instance, are small wedges of the fruit.

Appetizers are known as tidbits when they are bite-sized pieces. Some examples of them are nuts, olives, chips, and cheese cubes. They are usually eaten with the fingers or speared with wooden picks. Tidbits are good for buffets and cocktail parties—fun for people to munch on while standing.

TILSIT CHEESE *(til' zit)*—A yellow, semi-hard cheese also known as Tilsiter. This cheese belongs to the same family as Edam, Gouda, and Muenster. It is made from whole or skim cow's milk in plants.

Tilsit cheese was first made by Dutch immigrants in the old part of Tilsit, now Sovetsk in that part of Russia which was once East Russia. Today, Tilsit cheese is made throughout the world.

Tilsit is distinguished by its light yellow color, small holes, and plastic texture. The flavor is mild to moderately sharp and is often compared to a mild Limburger in flavor. (See also *Cheese*.)

TIMBALE *(tim' buhl)*—1. A custard or creamed meat mixture baked in a small, round mold. 2. An edible mold or case that is filled with a creamed mixture.

Some timbales are sweet and some are spicy. Sweet ones are served as desserts; spicy ones, served as appetizers or main dishes. The filling in main dish timbales consists of a rich cream sauce with finely chopped meat, fish, cheese, or vegetables.

Use Tilsit cheese for an appetizer or dessert.

Chicken Timbales

½ cup chicken broth
3 eggs
1 3-ounce can mushrooms, drained
1 sprig parsley
1 slice dry bread, torn in pieces
1 cup cubed, cooked chicken

Put all ingredients in blender container; blend till smooth. (When necessary, stop blender and use rubber spatula to scrape down sides.)

Pour into four 5- or 6-ounce greased custard cups; set in shallow pan on oven rack. Pour hot water in pan, 1 inch deep. Bake at 325° till set, 45 to 50 minutes. Makes 4 servings.

Timbale cases are made of a number of foods. Macaroni, spaghetti, and rice can be formed into a deep, round shell. However, the type most commonly associated with timbale is a pastry case. These are made by dipping a special iron into a batter and then deep-frying the pastry. This makes a small, cup-shaped shell.

Swedish Timbale Cases

1 cup sifted all-purpose flour
1 tablespoon sugar
¼ teaspoon salt
1 cup milk
2 well-beaten eggs

Sift flour, sugar, and salt together. Add milk to eggs; gradually stir in flour mixture; beat till smooth. Heat timbale iron in deep, hot fat (375°) 2 minutes. Drain excess fat from iron; dip into batter to within ¼ inch of top. Return at once to hot fat. Fry till case is crisp and golden, and slips from iron. Turn upside down to drain. Reheat iron 1 minute; make next case. Makes about 2 dozen timbale cases. (If batter slips off, iron is too cold; if it sticks, iron is too hot.)

TIMBALE IRON—A utensil with a long handle and a small metal mold on the end. This mold is usually in a small cup shape, but attachments such as stars, butterflies, and drums are also available.

Timbale irons are used for making timbale cases. The mold is dipped into batter and then placed in hot oil. This cooks the batter to produce a pastry shell for creamed and custard mixtures.

TIN—A soft metal. Tin is applied in a thin coat over steel and iron to make cooking utensils. Tin-plated utensils are shiny like aluminum when new but do darken with use. Care should be taken not to scour tin-plated utensils harshly. This can remove part of the tin coating, thus, exposing the base metal, which might rust with use. (See also *Pots and Pans.*)

TIPSY CAKE—A dessert made of sponge cake soaked with wine or brandy. The cake may also have a custard filling and a topping of whipped cream and nuts.

TISANE *(ti zan')*—An herb-flavored tea. Tisane is a general name for teas made from leaves, stems, flowers, or seeds. Examples of tisanes are camomile tea and tea made from steeping rose hips or orange blossoms. Swooning ladies were once revived with the aroma of tisanes.

TOAST—1. A slice of bread that has been browned with heat. 2. To brown, crisp, or dry a food by exposing it to heat. Coconuts, nuts, and seeds are toasted to develop flavor and color.

Cinnamon Toast

Combine 4 parts sugar and 1 part ground cinnamon.* Toast bread; butter while hot and sprinkle with sugar-cinnamon mixture. Keep warm in slow oven till serving time.

*Keep sugar-cinnamon mixture in a large shaker so it's ready to use instantly.

TOASTER—A small electrical appliance that browns and warms foods. Toasters originally were only for toasting bread slices, but today, an array of foods for the toaster is on the market. Frozen waffles, muffins, and toaster pastries are examples of the products that are quickly and easily heated in the automatic toaster.

Toasters are designed with wells to hold the slices of food while the electric coils produce the heat necessary for cooking. There are one-, two-, three-, and four-well models. Generally, they have a heat register. When the food reaches the degree of doneness you set, it pops up. The toaster then turns off automatically.

Toasters should be cared for exactly as the manufacturer directs. Never use a fork or knife inside the wells, since the wires are in this region. Be sure to clean the crumbs from the tray weekly so the toaster will operate at its maximum efficiency. (See also *Appliance.*)

TOASTER-OVEN—A small electric appliance that has a broiling unit in the top and sometimes a unit in the bottom, with a heat control. A tray slides in and out below the heating unit. This unit toasts bread, rolls, and sandwiches.

An automatic toaster-oven turns off itself when the food is done. In some models the door opens and the tray comes out automatically, too.

Toaster-ovens that have a lower heating element double as a small oven. You can bake rolls, potatoes, or small meat pies in them. (See also *Appliance.*)

TODDY—1. A hot drink consisting of spirits, such as rum or whiskey, water, sugar, lemon, and sometimes spices. 2. In some tropical countries, an unfermented or fermented juice that is extracted from certain palm trees and consumed cold.

TOFFEE *(tô′ fē, tof′ ē)*—A hard candy that is similar to a brittle. Sometimes, the name toffee is given to taffy.

Toffee is made of sugar, often brown sugar, butter, and nuts. The toffee pieces are frequently spread with chocolate and sprinkled with chopped or toasted nuts. When other desserts such as cookies are made with this same flavor combination, they are sometimes called toffee.

You can either buy toffee bars or make them yourself for eating as desserts or snacks. You can also use toffee as an ingredient in recipes. Crush them and add to desserts or cookies for flavor and crunch. (See also *Candy.*)

Toffee Bars

    1 cup butter or margarine,
        softened
    1 cup brown sugar
    1 teaspoon vanilla
    2 cups sifted all-purpose flour
            • • •
    1 6-ounce package semisweet
        chocolate pieces (1 cup)
    1 cup chopped walnuts

Thoroughly cream the butter or margarine, brown sugar, and vanilla. Add the flour; mix well. Stir in semisweet chocolate pieces and chopped walnuts. Pat the cookie mixture into an *ungreased* 15½x10x1-inch baking pan. Bake at 350° for 15 to 18 minutes. While warm, cut into bars. Cool. Makes 48 bars.

TOKAY *(tō kā′)*—1. A large, red, oval grape. 2. A white wine that is named for the village, Tokaj, in Hungary.

Tokay grapes are used mainly for eating out-of-hand. They are also delicious with cheese, in fruit bowls, and in salads. When used in any of these ways, however, the seeds must be removed.

Tokay wine traditionally is made in Hungary. This is usually sweet but some dry wine is produced. The region in which Tokay is made is small, as a result, the bottles of this wine are rare.

A type of Tokay wine is also produced in California. This type is usually a blend of several sweet wines.

Sweet Tokay is served with desserts. It should be just cooled. Dry Tokay is an aperitif and dinner wine. This type is served well chilled. (See *Grape, Wines and Spirits* for additional information.)

TOMALLEY *(tom′ al′ ē)*—The greenish brown liver located near the head of a lobster. It should not be removed but cooked and eaten. The tomalley is considered a delicacy to eat with the lobster or included in a stuffing for the lobster.

TOM AND JERRY—A hot alcoholic beverage that is made with rum, brandy, milk, eggs, sugar, and nutmeg. This mixture is particularly enjoyed during the holiday seasons of Christmas and New Year's.

TOMATO

This vegetable has gone from rags to riches in its popularity as a food.

Through the centuries, tomatoes have had so many exotic labels, such as *tomatl, pomi d'oro* (apples of gold), and *pomme d'amour* (love apples), that it is hard to believe that these juicy, flavorful fruits were regarded as poisonous for such a long time. Some of the folklore associated with tomatoes existed in the United States into the early-twentieth century.

Although it is only in recent years that tomatoes have been widely cultivated for food in the United States, it hasn't taken them long to become an integral part of our cooking heritage. Just think how incomplete some of your meals would be if tomatoes weren't there. Tossed salads wouldn't be quite the same without wedges of succulent tomatoes. And you would have to serve bacon and lettuce sandwiches tomatoless and spaghetti and pizza sauces without the red wonders. The list of tomato recipes is endless.

It was the South American Indians of long ago who first learned that tomatoes had food value. They cultivated wild tomato plants that grew in the regions of Peru, Bolivia, and Ecuador. Some of these Indians took tomatoes with them when they migrated north to Central America and Mexico, where the Mayans and Aztecs named tomatoes *tomatl.* With the exploration of the Americas by the Spanish came the introduction of tomatoes into Europe. It was not long before these fruits were an integral part

of the Spanish and Italian cuisines. The tomatoes they used, however, were not the same red-colored tomatoes that are familiar to us today. The Italians called them *pomi d'oro* (apples of gold), indicating that these varieties were yellow.

While the Spanish and Italians developed ways to use tomatoes extensively, other nationalities in Europe refused to accept them as food, believing tomatoes either to be poisonous or an aphrodisiac. The French named them *pomme d'amour*, love apples, because of tomatoes' so-called aphrodisiacal properties.

Tomatoes were shunned by many Americans, too. Although Thomas Jefferson grew and used tomatoes in the late 1700s, and the Creoles of Louisiana incorporated them into their cuisine early in the 1800s, it was not until the mid 1800s through the early 1900s that the folklore began to diminish.

The caution with which people accepted tomatoes stems from their relationship with the nightshade plant family. It has long been known that, when consumed, many of the members of this family are deadly poisonous. Since tomatoes are fruits of a perennial tropical vine belonging to the nightshade group, it is quite apparent how the old taboos started.

Today, there are many kinds of tomatoes. Some were developed for specific uses; others are enjoyed in many ways. The favorites are the red ones, but there are also yellows, greens, off-whites, and varicoloreds, all of which are popular. Just as there are many different colored tomatoes, so, too, are there different sizes and shapes. There are tomatoes as small as cherries and as large as pumpkins. There are round, pear-shaped, and oblong ones.

A fruit and vegetable

← Juicy goodness develops from each dainty, yellow blossom on the tomato vine, whether it's a miniature or a giant tomato variety.

How tomatoes are produced: After potatoes, tomatoes are the most commercially important vegetable in the United States. They are grown in every state when the weather permits. Tomatoes sold fresh to food markets come primarily from Texas, California, Florida, New Jersey, New York, and Maryland. Those grown for processing are raised mainly in California, Indiana, Maryland, New Jersey, Ohio, and Pennsylvania.

There are two major methods of production used today: the standard method and hydroponic growing. In either case, tomato plants, which are susceptible to cold weather, must be planted after danger of frost is past, although in the far south they can be grown during much of the winter season. At harvest time, tomatoes can be picked when mature but still green, or they can be allowed to ripen on the vine (usually labeled vine-ripened tomatoes). The green tomatoes ripen in shipment or at the warehouse.

With the standard method of production, the tomato seeds are planted indoors or outdoors, depending on the region of the country in which they are grown. After the last frost, the tomato plants are replanted in the fields. Some plants are allowed to vine out while other tomato plants are staked.

For hydroponic growing, seeds are sown in large tanks filled with soil and pebbles. The tanks are flooded with water to which nutrients have been added. Then, after a specified period, the water is pumped out. This procedure is repeated many times during the plants' growing cycle. Although production costs are higher with this method, the yield is increased greatly.

Nutritional value: The amount of nutrients obtained from tomatoes depends on whether they are fresh or canned, and vine-ripened or storage-ripened. Some nutrient values are increased by processing, while other values are decreased.

Fresh tomatoes are low in calories, but processed tomatoes vary according to the concentration of the product and the addition of ingredients. One medium raw tomato contains about 35 calories; ½ cup cooked, 25 calories; and ½ cup tomato juice, 20 calories. On the other hand, catsup, a concentrated, sweetened product, contains 20 calories per tablespoon.

Fresh tomatoes are good sources of vitamins A and C, and they are low in sodium. Other vitamins and minerals are present in small amounts, too. The vitamin and mineral value of vine-ripened tomatoes is better than that of artificially ripened tomatoes and canned tomatoes. The canning process reduces the vitamin C content to some degree, although there is still a fair amount of this nutrient.

Types of tomatoes: Although home growers usually prefer one tomato variety over another, such as Big Boy or Rutgers, varieties that are found in the supermarket are usually not designated. One type that has grown in popularity, however, is the miniature, bright red cherry tomato. Cherry tomatoes are excellent for eating raw, pickled, or preserved. They make a colorful addition to salads and are a good garnish for meat platters.

How to select

Both fresh and canned tomatoes are available during the entire year. Price differential between the two varies with the season of the year. In the summer when fresh tomatoes are plentiful, they may be a cheaper buy than canned ones.

The best-flavored fresh tomatoes are still the homegrown ones, which, to you, may be available at a nearby road stand or farm. The ultimate use of the tomatoes should largely determine the size and quality that you select—jumbos are best for stuffing, medium to large ones for slicing and small ones for cooking.

Look for ripe tomatoes with a good, plump shape and smooth, blemish-free skins. Fully ripe tomatoes are slightly soft to the touch. Avoid overripe, bruised, sunburned (green or yellow areas near stem ends), or decayed tomatoes. Water-soaked spots, depressed areas, and scars are all signs of poor quality and quite often result in unnecessary waste.

When you are selecting canned tomatoes, read the label carefully. Most canned tomatoes are peeled and packed in their own juice, but some may have pulp or semisolid paste added. Often, a grade determined by the United States Department of Agriculture appears on the label, although this grading is not mandatory.

There are five major USDA grades for tomatoes: U.S. Grade A (Fancy), U.S. Grade A Whole (Fancy Whole), U.S. Grade A, U.S. Grade B, and U.S. Grade C (Standard). Tomatoes falling in the first two categories are practically free of defects, peel, and core. These two differ in that the U.S. Grade Whole is a special pack containing more whole tomatoes. Both types are best used for salads, vegetable plates, and frying. The last three grades show a gradual decrease in identifiable tomato shape and an increase in permissible defects. The lower grades are better for stewing or cooking, where shape is not as important as it is for other uses.

How to store

All canned tomato products are shelf-stable. Their use need only be cycled within one year. Fresh tomatoes, on the other hand, require more timely care.

Dos and don'ts of ripening tomatoes

Do: Allow underripe tomatoes to fully ripen before refrigerating.

Ripen at moderate room temperatures (60° to 70°).

Set tomatoes out of direct sunlight.

Don't: Refrigerate underripe tomatoes.

Hold tomatoes at low temperatures (below 55°) to prolong ripening. Flavor and juiciness will not develop properly.

Place tomatoes in a sunny location. Sunlight inhibits normal color and flavor development.

Try to ripen green tomatoes.

If the fresh tomatoes are not fully ripe at the time of purchase, they should be kept in a warm place (60° to 70°) out of direct light until the proper ripeness develops. When the tomatoes are at the ripe stage, they should be stored in the vegetable crisper of the refrigerator. Refrigerated fresh tomatoes maintain their quality for two to five days.

Tomato skins slip off with ease when the tomato is immersed in a pan of boiling water for ½ minute, then into cold water.

For tomato roses, place stem end down. Cut 5 or 6 petals, cutting through skin but not seed pockets. Separate petals gently.

How to prepare

Tomatoes are a well-liked vegetable not only because of their flavor but because they are so easy to prepare – raw or cooked. Be sure to wash tomatoes before use, then peel, if desired, and serve as is or cooked. Peeling tomatoes is not a time-consuming project. Either dip the tomato in boiling water for ½ minute, then in cold water, or spear the tomato with a fork and rotate it over an open flame on the range till the skin wrinkles slightly.

For a stewed tomato mixture, peel and cut out tomato stems. Slowly cook whole or cut-up tomatoes in a covered pan without added water for 10 to 15 minutes. Season with salt, pepper, sugar, and, if desired, onion or various herbs and spices.

When the bounty of summer tomatoes is at hand, you can process tomatoes at home with relative ease. They do not freeze well because of their high water content, but they are a very popular vegetable to can. Use either the hot- or cold-pack method. Be certain to process them in the appropriate manner to ensure sterilization. (See also *Canning*.)

How to use

The versatility of tomatoes is reflected in the numerous seasonings that complement and highlight their flavor as well as the many ways in which they are used. Basil, bay leaf, chili powder, oregano, and thyme are used in varying combinations to give foreign influence (Italian, Spanish, or Mexican) to tomato-based foods. Other flavors that produce invigorating taste are caraway seed, celery seed, cloves, dill, rosemary, sage, and sesame seed. If the tomato flavor seems a bit too sharp, add a dash of sugar to mellow the acidity.

Tomato Topper

Blend ½ cup butter or margarine, softened; ¼ cup finely chopped, seeded, fresh tomato; dash dried basil leaves, crushed; and dash freshly ground pepper. Serve topper on cooked green beans, cauliflower, or lima beans.

Dill-Sauced Tomatoes

  ½ cup dairy sour cream
  ¼ cup mayonnaise or salad dressing
  2 tablespoons finely chopped onion
  ¼ teaspoon dried dillweed *or*
      1 teaspoon snipped, fresh dill
  ¼ teaspoon salt
        • • •
  3 large, firm, ripe tomatoes
    Salt and pepper
    Butter or margarine

Combine sour cream, mayonnaise, onion, dill, and the ¼ teaspoon salt; mix well. Chill. Core tomatoes and cut in half crosswise. Season the cut surfaces with salt and pepper; dot the tomatoes with butter or margarine.

Broil, cut side up, 3 inches from heat till heated through, about 5 minutes. Spoon sauce over broiled tomatoes. Makes 6 servings.

Svengali Tomatoes

A unique seasoning blend—

In a saucepan combine 1 16-ounce can tomatoes, cut up; ¼ cup canned or frozen cranberry-orange relish; 2 tablespoons light raisins; 1 tablespoon sugar; ½ teaspoon *each* salt and ground ginger; and ¼ teaspoon cayenne. Simmer 8 to 10 minutes. Serve warm or chilled.

Herbed Tomatoes

  6 ripe tomatoes, peeled and
      sliced
  1 teaspoon salt
  ¼ teaspoon freshly ground
      pepper
  ½ teaspoon dried thyme leaves *or*
      marjoram leaves, crushed
  ¼ cup finely snipped parsley
  ¼ cup snipped chives
  ⅔ cup salad oil
  ¼ cup tarragon vinegar

Place the tomatoes in a bowl; sprinkle with the seasonings and herbs. Combine oil and vinegar; pour over. Cover; chill 3 hours, spooning dressing over a few times. Drain off the dressing and pass with the tomatoes.

Juicy, fully ripe tomatoes are unbeatable when they are sliced and served as a vegetable side dish. Add a marinade or perky salad dressing if your family likes. Petite cherry tomatoes make excellent dippers for appetizer dips and dunks and are also good salad fare. Full-sized tomatoes are salad musts, too—in tossed combos or left whole and stuffed with a robust salad mixture.

Bean-Stuffed Tomatoes

- 1 9-ounce package frozen Italian green beans
- ¼ cup sliced green onion
- 1 3-ounce can broiled, sliced mushrooms, drained (½ cup)
- ⅓ cup Italian salad dressing
- 6 medium tomatoes

Cook beans according to package directions; drain thoroughly. Add onion, mushrooms, salad dressing, ¼ teaspoon salt, and dash pepper; toss till beans are coated. Refrigerate at least 2 hours, stirring occasionally.

Meanwhile, cut thin slice from top of each tomato. Using a small spoon, scoop out centers, leaving shells about ¼ inch thick. (Use tomato centers in sauce or salad another time.) Invert shells on paper toweling to drain; chill. At serving time, sprinkle inside of tomato shells with salt; spoon in bean mixture. Serves 6.

Bacon, Lettuce, and Tomato Salad

Make croutons by toasting 1 cup ½-inch bread cubes at 225° till dry, about 2 hours. Line salad bowl with romaine. In salad bowl combine toasted bread cubes; 3 cups torn lettuce (½ medium head); 3 medium tomatoes, cut in wedges; 8 slices bacon, crisp-cooked, drained, and crumbled; and ½ cup mayonnaise or salad dressing. Toss. Season. Serves 4 or 5.

Serve with steak

Bean-Stuffed Tomatoes are transformed into a diet feature by replacing regular Italian salad dressing with the low-calorie form.

Stuffed Tomatoes

Cut tomatoes in Cups, Fantans, or Daisies. At serving time, salt cut surfaces; fill.

Cup: Peel the tomato, if desired. Cut thin slice from the top; scoop out center. Invert on paper toweling and chill.

Fantan: Turn tomato stem end down. Cut down to *but not through* bottom, making 5 slices. Invert tomato on paper toweling. Chill.

Daisy: Turn tomato stem end down. Cut down *to but not through* the bottom in 5 or 6 wedges. Scoop out some of the center. Invert tomato on paper toweling and chill.

Tomato Fillings

Tuna or any seafood salad. Serve with lemon wedges; trim with some parsley.

Ham, egg, or chicken salad.

In a bowl combine 2 cups cream-style cottage cheese, 1 cup shredded sharp process American cheese, ½ cup sliced pimiento-stuffed green olives, and ¼ cup chopped walnuts. Makes enough filling for 6 to 8 tomatoes.

Shrimp–Rice Salad

     6 large tomatoes
     2 cups cleaned, peeled, cooked
        shrimp, cut up
  1½ cups cooked rice
     ⅓ cup chopped celery
     ¼ cup sliced, pitted ripe olives
     1 tablespoon snipped parsley
     ¼ cup salad oil
     2 tablespoons red wine vinegar
     1 small clove garlic, minced
     ¼ teaspoon dry mustard
     ¼ teaspoon paprika

With the stem ends down, cut the tomatoes into 6 wedges, *cutting to, but not through* bases. Spread the wedges apart slightly. Carefully scoop out pulp; dice and drain pulp. Chill tomato shells. Combine diced tomato, shrimp, rice, celery, olives, and parsley.

Blend remaining ingredients and ½ teaspoon salt; toss with shrimp mixture. Season with salt and pepper. Chill. Just before serving, spoon into shells. If desired, trim with watercress and additional shrimp. Serves 6.

Quick Tuna Salad

Combine one 16-ounce can macaroni and cheese; one 6½- or 7-ounce can tuna, drained and flaked; one 8-ounce can peas, drained; ⅓ cup mayonnaise; 2 hard-cooked eggs, chopped; 1 tablespoon chopped green pepper; 1 teaspoon instant minced onion; ¼ teaspoon salt; and dash pepper. Chill the mixture thoroughly.

Cut 6 chilled medium tomatoes in sixths, to within ½ inch of bottom. Spread wedges apart. Sprinkle inside of each tomato with salt, then fill with salad. Makes 6 servings.

Sandwiches take on a colorful appearance with the help of sliced tomatoes and lettuce. Summertime treats include the famous b-l-t (bacon, lettuce, and tomato) as well as tomato-topped hamburgers in buns and grilled cheese sandwiches.

Cooked versions of tomatoes range from appetizers to hearty main dishes. Both green and red tomatoes are the bases for relishes mixtures. By themselves, they can be baked, broiled, or fried. Add a topping of buttered bread crumbs, snipped parsley, or melted cheese to baked or broiled tomatoes. Serve fried ones over toast with savory cream sauce.

Dilly Green Tomatoes

  3½ pounds small, firm green tomatoes
        with stems
     4 cloves garlic
     4 stalks celery
     4 red chili peppers
     4 heads fresh dill *or* 4 teaspoons
        dried dillweed *or* 8 tablespoons
        dillseed
     1 quart cider vinegar
     ½ cup granulated pickling salt

Wash tomatoes; drain. Pack into hot quart jars. To *each quart* add 1 clove garlic, 1 stalk celery, 1 pepper, and 1 head fresh dill *or* 1 teaspoon dillweed *or* 2 tablespoons dillseed.

Combine 2 quarts water, vinegar, and salt. Bring to boiling; fill hot jars to within ½ inch of top. Adjust lids. Process in boiling water bath for 5 minutes (start counting time when water returns to boil). Makes 4 quarts.

Baked Tomatoes

Place the tomato halves in a shallow baking pan. Sprinkle the tomatoes with seasoned salt and buttered cracker crumbs, if desired. Bake at 375° for about 20 minutes.

Broiled Tomatoes

Broil tomato halves, cut side up, 3 inches from heat till hot through, about 5 minutes (don't turn). If desired, dot with butter, season to taste with salt and pepper, and sprinkle with crushed herbs before broiling. *Or* combine ½ cup dairy sour cream, ¼ cup mayonnaise, 2 tablespoons finely chopped onion, ¼ teaspoon dried dillweed, and ¼ teaspoon salt. Spoon over hot, broiled tomatoes.

Fried Tomatoes

Cut unpeeled *green* tomatoes in ½-inch slices. Dip in seasoned flour. Brown *slowly* in hot fat on both sides. *Or* dip ½-inch *ripe* tomato slices into beaten egg mixed with water, then into fine dry bread or cracker crumbs. Fry *quickly* in hot fat; season with salt and pepper.

Deviled Baked Tomatoes

Zesty crumb topping—

   2 medium ripe tomatoes
   1 teaspoon prepared mustard
   ¼ cup minced onion
   ¼ cup buttered soft bread crumbs
   ½ teaspoon Worcestershire sauce
       Dash salt

Remove stems from tomatoes; halve crosswise. Arrange the tomatoes, cut sides up, in a 10x 6x1¾-inch baking dish. Spread with mustard; combine onion, buttered bread crumbs, Worcestershire sauce, and salt. Sprinkle the mixture over tomatoes. Bake at 375° till heated through, about 20 minutes. Makes 4 servings.

Baked or stewed tomatoes and tomato-vegetable mixtures put flair into mealtime. Tomatoes are tempting with many garden-fresh vegetables. Season with butter, salt, and pepper, or spice up the dish with sour cream, a tangy vinegar-based dressing, or cheese sauce.

Tomato Casserole

   1 medium onion, chopped
   2 tablespoons butter or margarine
   4 medium ripe tomatoes, sliced
   1 cup shredded sharp process
       American cheese
   1 cup fine soft bread crumbs
   1 cup dairy sour cream
   2 well-beaten eggs

Cook onion in butter till tender. Place *half* the tomatoes in a 10x6x1¾-inch baking dish. Top with *half each* onion, cheese, and crumbs; repeat. Mix sour cream, eggs, and ½ teaspoon salt. Pour over top; cover. Bake at 350° for 30 minutes. Uncover; bake 10 minutes. Serves 6.

Tomatoes with French Dressing

Cut thin slice from tops of 4 medium ripe tomatoes. Hollow out slightly. Combine ¼ cup salad oil, 1½ tablespoons cider vinegar, ¼ teaspoon Worcestershire sauce, 1 tablespoon sugar, 1½ teaspoons instant minced onion, ¼ teaspoon salt, and ¼ teaspoon dry mustard. Spoon into center of each tomato.

Mix ⅓ cup medium fine cracker crumbs and 1 tablespoon butter, melted. Sprinkle over tomatoes. Place in 9x1½-inch round pan. Bake at 350° 30 minutes. Serves 4.

Tomato Sauerkraut

   ½ cup sliced onion
   2 tablespoons butter or margarine
   1 tablespoon all-purpose flour
   1 27-ounce can sauerkraut,
       drained (3½ cups)
   1½ cups tomato juice
   1 bay leaf, crushed
   ⅓ cup brown sugar

Cook onion in butter till tender. Blend in flour. Stir in remaining ingredients and ½ teaspoon salt. Cover; simmer 30 minutes.

Tomato pieces or purée used in tomato soup, vegetable soups, or meat-based stews add flattering color and flavor.

Hot Tomato Bouillon

1 10½-ounce can condensed tomato soup
1 10½-ounce can condensed beef broth
1⅓ cups water
¼ cup acini di pepe (solid dots)
½ teaspoon prepared horseradish

• • •

1 small avocado, peeled and sliced and/or 2 slices bacon, crisp-cooked, drained, and crumbled

In saucepan combine condensed tomato soup, condensed beef broth, water, acini di pepe, and prepared horseradish. Bring mixture to boiling; simmer till pasta is tender, 7 to 10 minutes, stirring occasionally. Float avocado slices and/or crisp-cooked, crumbled bacon atop bouillon. Makes 4 servings.

Tomato-Rice Soup

In saucepan cook ½ cup long-grain rice and ¼ cup diced celery in 4 cups chicken broth till rice is tender. Add one 10¾-ounce can condensed tomato soup, 1 dried whole red chili, and salt to taste. Heat through. Remove chili. Serve the soup hot. Makes 6 servings.

The list of main dishes in which tomatoes are used astounds the imagination. Whole tomatoes are hollowed out and stuffed with savory meat mixtures. Tomato wedges alternate on exotic meat-and-vegetable kabobs. Saucy tomato mixtures and casseroles are good, too.

Star at a luncheon

← Wedged tomatoes separate enough to hold chilly Shrimp-Rice Salad. Line each serving with watercress and garnish with shrimp.

Mexican Mix-Ups

1 16-ounce can tomatoes
1 15-ounce can tamales, cut in bite-sized pieces
1 15-ounce can chili with beans
1 12-ounce can whole kernel corn, undrained
Shredded sharp natural Cheddar cheese
Corn chips

In large saucepan combine tomatoes, tamales, chili, and corn. Simmer, uncovered, for 25 to 30 minutes. Spoon into serving bowls. Top *each* serving with about 2 tablespoons cheese. Pass corn chips. Makes 4 to 6 servings.

Italian Meat Sauce

1 cup chopped onion
1 pound ground beef
2 cloves garlic, minced
1 30-ounce can tomatoes, cut up
1 16-ounce can tomatoes, cut up
1 6-ounce can tomato paste
¼ cup snipped parsley
1 tablespoon brown sugar
1 teaspoon salt
1½ teaspoons dried oregano leaves, crushed
¼ teaspoon dried thyme leaves, crushed
1 bay leaf
Hot cooked spaghetti
Shredded Parmesan cheese

In Dutch oven combine onion, meat, and garlic; cook till meat is browned and onion is tender. Skim off excess fat; add 2 cups water and next 9 ingredients.

Simmer, uncovered, till sauce is thick, about 3 hours; stir occasionally. Remove bay leaf. Serve over hot spaghetti. Pass bowl of shredded Parmesan cheese. Makes 6 servings.

Tomato products

A large portion of the tomatoes that are commercially grown in the United States are transported to the canner and processed into various tomato products within a few hours of harvest. Tomato catsup, juice, paste, purée, sauce, and chili sauce all encompass a wide range of available forms of tomatoes.

Tomato catsup: A thick, semiliquid tomato sauce used as a condiment. Some catsup contains an assortment of seasonings and spices as determined by the manufacturer. Consistencies also vary with the producer. Select as desired.

Saucy Bean Burgers

    1 pound ground beef
    1 11½-ounce can condensed
        bean with bacon soup
    ½ cup catsup
    ¼ cup water
    8 hamburger buns, split and
        toasted

In skillet brown beef; drain. Add soup, catsup, and water. Cook and stir till boiling, about 5 minutes. Serve in buns. Makes 8 servings.

Tomato juice: A full-strength juice strained from tomato pulp. No additional water is used. Tomato juice contains no added seasonings except salt. Specially seasoned tomato juices are marketed under separate names, such as vegetable juice cocktail, and not tomato juice.

Barbecue Bean Soup

Each serving is cheese-topped—

    ½ pound ground beef
    ½ cup chopped onion
    1 18-ounce can tomato juice
    1 16-ounce can barbecue beans
    1 cup water
    2 ounces sharp process American
        cheese, shredded (½ cup)

In large saucepan cook beef with onion till meat is browned and onion is tender; drain off fat. Add tomato juice, barbecue beans, and water. Simmer, covered, for 10 minutes. Spoon into soup bowls; sprinkle each serving with shredded cheese. Makes 6 servings.

Hot Tomato Cocktail

    1 46-ounce can tomato juice
        (about 6 cups)
    1 10½-ounce can condensed beef
        broth
    1 teaspoon grated onion
    1 teaspoon prepared horseradish
    1 teaspoon Worcestershire sauce
    1 or 2 drops bottled hot pepper
        sauce
        • • •
    8 lemon twists
    8 cocktail onions

In blazer pan of chafing dish combine tomato juice, beef broth, onion, horseradish, Worcestershire sauce, and hot pepper sauce. Heat just to boiling. Ladle into cups. Garnish each serving with a twist of lemon and cocktail onion speared on a cocktail pick. Makes 8 servings.

Vegetable Cocktail Soup

    1 10½-ounce can condensed beef
        broth
    1 12-ounce can vegetable juice
        cocktail

Combine broth and juice. Serve immediately over cracked ice. Makes 4 or 5 servings.

Tomato paste: An extremely thick, paste-like tomato concentrate. No seasoning is added except salt. In cooking, tomato paste is usually diluted with water.

Tomato purée: An unseasoned, strained tomato concentrate that is more liquid in consistency than is tomato paste; thus, it pours quite readily.

Tomato sauce: Puréed tomatoes to which seasonings have been added. The seasonings include salt, pepper, herbs, and spices, which vary in concentration and proportion from one manufacturer to another. In recent years, improvements in processing techniques have enabled further diversification of tomato sauces, including the addition of food pieces such as onions, mushrooms, and cheeses.

Tomato Dressing

    1 8-ounce can tomato sauce
    2 tablespoons tarragon vinegar
    1 teaspoon onion juice
    1 teaspoon Worcestershire sauce
    ½ teaspoon salt
    ½ teaspoon dried dillweed
    ½ teaspoon dried basil leaves,
        crushed

Combine tomato sauce, vinegar, onion juice, Worcestershire sauce, salt, dillweed, and basil in screw-top jar. Cover and shake well. Chill. Shake before serving. Makes 1 cup.

Beef Roll-Ups

    2 pounds round steak, cut ¼ inch
        thick
    3 tablespoons prepared mustard
    ¼ cup finely minced onion
    4 strips bacon, cut in half
    1 large dill pickle, cut in 8
        lengthwise strips
    2 tablespoons all-purpose flour
    1½ teaspoons salt
    ⅛ teaspoon pepper
    3 tablespoons salad oil
    1 8-ounce can tomato sauce (1 cup)
    1 teaspoon Worcestershire sauce
    1 teaspoon beef-flavored gravy
        base
    1 teaspoon brown sugar
        Hot, buttered noodles

Cut round steak in 8 rectangular pieces; spread prepared mustard on meat to within ½ inch of edge. Sprinkle with onion. Top with half of the strips of bacon and the pickle strips. Roll up jelly-roll fashion, tucking in edges. Tie with heavy cord, or skewer securely.

Combine flour, salt, and pepper; coat roll-ups with mixture and brown slowly on all sides in hot oil. Combine tomato sauce, Worcestershire sauce, beef gravy base, 1 cup hot water, and brown sugar; pour over meat. Cover and simmer for about 1¼ hours. Remove the meat from the sauce; cut cord or remove skewers.

Thicken sauce with a little flour paste (1 to 2 tablespoons flour dissolved in an equal amount of cold water), if necessary. Serve over hot, buttered noodles; top with sauce. Serves 8.

Versatile tomato products—sauce, purée, and paste.

Lamb-Eggplant Balls

Simmered in tomato sauce—

Combine 1 beaten egg; ⅓ cup soft bread crumbs (½ slice); 2 cups chopped, peeled eggplant; ½ cup chopped onion; 1 teaspoon snipped parsley; 1 teaspoon salt; and ⅛ teaspoon pepper. Add 1½ pounds ground lamb and mix well. Shape into 18 meatballs. In a skillet brown the meatballs in oil. Drain.

Blend one 8-ounce can tomato sauce and ⅛ teaspoon dry mustard; pour over balls. Simmer, covered, for 30 minutes. Uncover; cook 15 minutes more. Makes 6 servings.

Pizza Wheels

    1 beaten egg
    ⅓ cup milk
    ⅓ cup fine dry bread crumbs
    ⅓ cup finely chopped onion
    ¾ teaspoon salt
    2 pounds ground beef
    1 8-ounce can tomato sauce
    1 3-ounce can chopped mushrooms,
        drained and finely chopped
    ¾ teaspoon dried basil leaves,
        crushed
    3 slices mozzarella cheese, cut
        in strips

Combine first 5 ingredients. Add meat; mix well. In shallow baking pan shape into 7 or 8 circles, about 4 to 4½ inches in diameter, building a 1-inch-high edge. Combine tomato sauce, mushrooms, and basil; spoon into patties. Bake at 375° for 30 minutes. Lay the cheese strips spoke-fashion atop pizzas. Bake for 2 minutes. Makes 7 or 8 servings.

Beef Goulash and Noodles

Brown 2 pounds beef chuck, cut in ¾-inch cubes, in ⅓ cup shortening. Add 1 cup chopped onion; cook till tender. Stir in 1 tablespoon *each* all-purpose flour and paprika and 1 teaspoon salt. Add one 8-ounce can tomato sauce; one 16-ounce can tomatoes; 1 or 2 cloves garlic, minced, and Bouquet Garni. Cover; simmer about 1½ hours. Remove Bouquet Garni.

Add 2 tablespoons *each* poppy seed and butter to 6 ounces medium egg noodles, cooked. Serve goulash over noodles. Serves 6 to 8.

Bouquet Garni: In cheesecloth, tie 1 bay leaf; 1 stalk celery, cut up; 2 tablespoons parsley; and ¼ teaspoon dried thyme, crushed.

Chili sauce: A catsuplike condiment that retains the tomato seeds. It is pulpier than is catsup due to the inclusion of chopped vegetables such as onion, pepper, and celery. (See also *Vegetable*.)

Mexican Hot Sauce

Combine 1 cup chili sauce; ¼ cup chopped onion; 3 tablespoons vinegar; 1 tablespoon salad oil; 1 teaspoon brown sugar; 1 clove garlic, crushed; ¼ teaspoon salt; ¼ teaspoon dry mustard; and ¼ teaspoon bottled hot pepper sauce. Bring to boiling. Simmer 10 minutes, stirring occasionally. Makes 1¼ cups.

A seasoning-blended tomato sauce coats tender Beef Roll-Ups as they rest on a bed of hot buttered noodles. Strips of dill pickle and bacon hide inside each hearty meat serving.

TOMCOD—A small fish similar to the cod. This "Tom Thumb" of the cod family lives in the Atlantic and Pacific oceans. (See *Cod, Fish* for additional information.)

TONGUE—The edible meat from beef, veal, lamb, or pork tongue. Tongue is available in fresh, pickled (corned), cured and smoked, and canned forms. Beef tongue is the type most commonly available in all forms. Most pork and lamb tongue has been cooked by the meat packer and is sold in ready-to-serve forms.

The size of the tongue is directly related to the type of animal from which it comes. Beef tongues usually range from two to five pounds; lamb tongues weigh only a few ounces. Pork and veal tongues fall in between these two extremes.

A 3-ounce cooked portion of tongue provides about 220 calories and many essential nutrients. It is a good source of protein and the B vitamin complex.

Tongue, like other variety meats, is more perishable than are other meat cuts. Fresh tongue should be refrigerator stored and cooked within a day. Smoked and pickled (corned) tongue will keep in the refrigerator a day or two longer.

Tongue is not a tender meat and needs long, slow cooking in liquid to make it tender. Except for canned tongue, all forms are cooked, covered, in enough simmering water to cover. Add 1 teaspoon salt for each quart of water when cooking fresh tongue. Spices such as peppercorns, cloves, and bay leaves or vegetables such as carrots, onion, and celery can be added to the cooking liquid. Allow a cooking time of about 1 hour per pound of meat.

When the meat is tender, plunge the tongue in cold water to help loosen the skin. When cool enough to handle, cut away any gristle and bits of bone. On the underside, cut the skin lengthwise from large end to tip, being careful not to cut into tongue. Loosen the skin at the thick end with a knife, then peel off the skin. If there are areas of skin that adhere more firmly, make several lengthwise slits with a knife and remove the skin in strips.

Cooked tongue is usually bias-sliced thinly and served hot or cold. Tomato, sweet-sour, brown, and white sauces complement hot tongue as toppings for the sliced meat or in casseroles and skillet dishes featuring tongue. Cold tongue slices are perfect for cold meat platters, sandwiches, and salads. When served cold, the meat will be more moist if cooled in the cooking liquid. One pound of meat serves four people. (See also *Variety Meat.*)

Ginger-Sauced Tongue

    1 2- to 4-pound smoked beef
        tongue
    1 medium onion, sliced
    1 teaspoon whole cloves
    1 teaspoon whole peppercorns
    4 bay leaves
        Gingersnap Sauce

Place meat in Dutch oven; cover with water. Add next 4 ingredients. Cover and simmer till tender; allow 1 hour *per pound*. Remove meat; strain, reserving 1 cup liquid. Cut off bones and gristle from large end. Slit skin on underside; peel off. Slice meat on a slant.

Serve with hot *Gingersnap Sauce:* Crush 5 gingersnaps; combine with 1/3 cup brown sugar, 1/3 cup raisins, 1/4 cup vinegar, and reserved liquid. Cook and stir till smooth. Makes about 4 servings per pound.

Tongue and Bean Skillet

    2 tablespoons chopped onion
    1 tablespoon butter or margarine
    1 beef bouillon cube
    2 teaspoons cornstarch
  1/3 cup catsup
            • • •
  1/8 teaspoon dried thyme leaves,
        crushed
    2 cups thinly sliced, cooked
        beef tongue
    1 10-ounce package frozen baby
        lima beans, cooked and drained

In skillet cook onion in butter till tender but not brown. Dissolve bouillon cube in 3/4 cup boiling water. Blend cornstarch and catsup. Stir into bouillon. Add thyme. Combine with cooked onion, tongue, and beans. Simmer about 5 minutes. Makes 4 or 5 servings.

Cheesy Tongue on Rice

      8 ounces sharp process American
          cheese, shredded (2 cups)
    ½ teaspoon dry mustard
    ¾ cup milk
    ½ teaspoon Worcestershire sauce
          Dash cayenne
      1 well-beaten egg
    1½ cups cooked tongue, cut in thin
          strips 3 inches long
          Hot cooked rice

In saucepan toss cheese with mustard. Add milk. Stir over low heat till cheese melts and and is smooth. Stir in Worcestershire sauce and cayenne. Stir small amount of hot mixture into egg. Return to hot mixture. Stir in tongue. Cook and stir over low heat till mixture is thick and creamy. Serve over rice. Serves 4.

The exotic fig-date flavor of Tropical Fruit Topper is equally good served warm or cold over scoops of sherbet or ice cream.

TONIC WATER—Another name for carbonated quinine water that is used as a drink mixer. (See also *Quinine Water*.)

TOPPING—A food used for a decorative and/or flavor touch that is placed atop another food. Some toppings are as simple as confectioners' sugar dusted on top of gingerbread, chopped nuts sprinkled on cookies, or ground nutmeg dashed atop custard. Others, such as the biscuit and potato toppings for casseroles, syrups for pancakes and waffles, and sauces for ice cream sundaes, are recipes themselves. Here are some creative topping recipes that make foods look pretty and taste delicious.

Tropical Fruit Topper

Combine 1 cup finely snipped, pitted dates with 1 cup water; ½ cup finely snipped figs; and ½ cup light corn syrup in small saucepan. Cook and stir over low heat till mixture thickens, about 15 to 20 minutes. Remove from heat; stir in ½ cup coarsely chopped pecans. Serve sauce warm or cool over sherbet or ice cream. Makes 1⅓ cups sauce.

Sunny Citrus-Cream Topping

      2 beaten eggs
    ¼ cup sugar
    ⅓ cup tangerine juice
          • • •
      1 teaspoon grated tangerine
          peel
      2 tangerines, peeled and
          sectioned
      1 cup whipping cream
          Flaked coconut

Combine eggs and sugar in a saucepan; stir in tangerine juice. Cook over low heat, stirring constantly, till mixture thickens, about 10 minutes. Remove the mixture from heat; add grated tangerine peel. Cool.

Reserve 8 to 10 tangerine sections for garnish. Cut remaining sections in small pieces; fold into egg mixture. Whip cream; fold into egg mixture. Garnish with reserved tangerine sections; sprinkle with coconut. Serve over waffles or unfrosted cake. Makes 3 cups.

TORTE *(tôrt)* — A rich cake or pastry. In the past, a torte was a flat, round cake. Today, the only basic requirement of a torte is that it be rich and delicious.

Variety is the key word when describing what a torte can be, as is evident from a look at some of the classic tortes. The Dobos torte is composed of layers of sponge cake, buttercream filling, and a caramel glaze. The Sacher torte has an apricot filling between cake layers and a chocolate glaze. The Schaum torte has meringue rather than cake layers, crushed fruit for a filling, and a whipped cream topping, while the Blitz torte has a meringuelike topping that is baked atop the cake layers.

Most tortes, however, have the following characteristics: (**1**) The basis for the torte is a meringue or a cake. The cakes are made with little or no flour. Crumbs or ground nuts may be substituted for the flour. (**2**) Leavening in the torte usually comes from air that is incorporated into the eggs. (**3**) A custard or fruit filling is used between the layers of meringue or cake. (**4**) The torte may have icing, whipped cream, or meringue for a frosting and a garnish of nuts or fruit.

With cake or meringue layers, a filling in between, and a frosting, a torte becomes a glamorous dessert. It will certainly impress your guests and make the family feel like royalty. To create this spectacular pastry, you can begin with basic ingredients (even grinding the nuts yourself), or you can use convenience products. Either way, you are sure to have a torte that will be a grand treat for all. (See also *Dessert*.)

Forgotten Cherry Torte

    5 egg whites
    ½ teaspoon cream of tartar
    ¼ teaspoon salt
    1½ cups sugar
    2 cups frozen whipped dessert
        topping, thawed
    1 21-ounce can cherry pie filling
    1 tablespoon lemon juice
        Several drops almond extract
        Frozen whipped dessert topping,
        thawed

Preheat oven to 450°. In mixer bowl beat egg whites till frothy. Add cream of tartar and salt; beat till soft peaks form. Gradually add sugar, a tablespoon at a time, beating till stiff peaks form. Turn meringue mixture into buttered 8x8x2-inch baking dish. Place in preheated oven. *Close oven door; immediately turn off heat. Leave oven door closed for 8 hours or overnight.* (Don't peek!)

Spread *1 cup* of the thawed, whipped dessert topping over the meringue. Combine cherry pie filling, lemon juice, and almond extract; spread *half* the pie filling mixture over topping in baking dish. Repeat layers with *1 cup* whipped dessert topping and remaining cherry filling mixture, spreading to cover edges.

Cover torte and chill overnight. Cut torte in 6 or 8 squares; top each square with a dollop of additional whipped dessert topping, if desired. Makes 6 to 8 servings.

Add a note of glamour to dessert by serving a torte. Chocolate-Cherry Torte is an example of this beautiful, delectable dessert.

Assemble Chocolate-Cherry Torte by putting a mound of frosting in the center of cake layer and by making a border for the filling.

Chocolate-Cherry Torte

1 package 2-layer-size chocolate cake mix
¼ cup granulated sugar
2 tablespoons cornstarch
  Dash salt
1 20-ounce can frozen, pitted tart red cherries, thawed
1 teaspoon rum extract

• • •

1 cup butter or margarine, softened
4½ cups sifted confectioners' sugar
2 2-ounce envelopes no-melt unsweetened chocolate
3 egg yolks

• • •

  Shaved chocolate
  Candied red cherries

Prepare chocolate cake mix according to package directions. Cool. Blend together granulated sugar, cornstarch, and salt. Stir in thawed, pitted tart red cherries. Cook over medium-low heat, stirring frequently, till thick and clear. Reduce heat; cook mixture 2 minutes more. Stir in rum extract. Chill thoroughly.

With electric mixer beat butter or margarine, confectioners' sugar, and no-melt unsweetened chocolate together till smooth. Add egg yolks, one at a time, beating after each addition till light and fluffy. Place four strips of waxed paper over edges of plate to protect from spatters. Place one cake layer on plate, flat side up. Fill a ½-cup measure with buttercream frosting; turn out on center of cake. With *1 cup* more of frosting, make ½-inch border around edge, same height as center frosting.

Spoon chilled cherry filling between border and center mound of frosting. Top with second cake layer; press lightly. Frost torte with remaining buttercream. Garnish top and sides of cake with shaved chocolate. Arrange candied red cherries around edge of cake. Remove waxed paper strips. Chill torte for several hours. Let stand at room temperature for 20 minutes before serving. Serves 12 to 16.

Surprise Chocolate Torte

8 egg yolks
1 teaspoon vanilla
1¼ cups sifted confectioners' sugar
½ cup unsweetened cocoa powder
8 egg whites
  Dash salt

• • •

2 cups whipping cream
3 tablespoons granulated sugar
1 tablespoon instant coffee powder
  Semisweet chocolate curls

In small mixer bowl beat egg yolks and vanilla till thick and lemon colored, about 5 minutes. Sift together confectioners' sugar and cocoa; blend into beaten egg yolks. Beat 1 minute more. Wash and dry beaters.

In large mixer bowl beat egg whites with salt till stiff peaks form. Carefully fold egg yolk mixture into egg whites. Pour into *ungreased* 9-inch springform pan. Bake at 325° till done, about 45 to 50 minutes. Remove from oven and cool on rack. *The center of the torte will fall.* Gently loosen torte from sides of pan; place torte on serving plate.

Combine whipping cream, granulated sugar, and coffee powder; whip till stiff. Spoon whipped mixture into center of torte. Garnish with chocolate curls. Makes 10 to 12 servings.

Chocolate-Pecan Torte

    1 6-ounce package semisweet
        chocolate pieces (1 cup)
    3 tablespoons butter or
        margarine
    9 egg yolks
    ½ cup sifted confectioners'
        sugar
    9 egg whites
    ¼ teaspoon salt
    ½ cup sifted confectioners'
        sugar
    3 cups ground pecans
      Cream Filling
      Chocolate Frosting

Melt together chocolate pieces and butter or margarine; cool to lukewarm. In small mixer bowl beat egg yolks till thick and lemon colored. Gradually add the first ½ cup confectioners' sugar. Stir in the cooled chocolate mixture. In large mixer bowl combine egg whites and salt; beat to soft peaks. Gradually add the remaining confectioners' sugar, beating to stiff peaks. Gently fold in the chocolate mixture and the ground pecans.

Turn into 3 greased and waxed-paper-lined 9x1½-inch round pans, dividing batter among pans. Bake at 325° for 30 minutes. Immediately loosen and remove from pans; cool on racks.

Spread Cream Filling between layers and Chocolate Frosting on sides and top of cake. Chill 2 hours. Makes 16 to 20 servings.

Cream Filling: In small saucepan gradually blend ½ cup milk into 2 tablespoons all-purpose flour till smooth. Cook and stir over low heat till thickened and smooth. Cool to room temperature, stirring frequently. Cream ½ cup butter or margarine, ½ cup granulated sugar, and ¼ teaspoon salt till light. Beat in the cooled flour mixture. Makes 1½ cups filling.

Chocolate Frosting: In medium saucepan melt two 1-ounce squares unsweetened chocolate over low heat. In small bowl combine 1 cup granulated sugar, ¼ cup cornstarch, and ¼ teaspoon salt. Stir into melted chocolate. Gradually add 1 cup *boiling* water, stirring till smooth. Cook and stir over low heat till thickened and smooth; remove from heat. Blend in 3 tablespoons butter or margarine and 1 teaspoon vanilla. Chill over ice water, stirring mixture occasionally, till thickened to spreading consistency. Makes 2 cups.

Chocolate Torte

    ¼ cup shortening
    1 cup granulated sugar
    2 egg yolks
    2 1-ounce squares unsweetened
        chocolate, melted
    1¼ cups sifted all-purpose flour
    ½ teaspoon salt
    ½ teaspoon baking powder
    ½ teaspoon baking soda
    ¾ cup milk
    1 teaspoon vanilla
    2 stiffly beaten egg whites
    8 1-ounce squares semisweet
        chocolate
    1 cup whipping cream
    ½ cup slivered, blanched almonds,
        toasted
    1½ 1-ounce squares unsweetened
        chocolate
    2 tablespoons butter or margarine
    1½ cups sifted confectioners'
        sugar
    1 teaspoon vanilla
      Boiling water

Stir shortening to soften. Gradually add granulated sugar, creaming thoroughly. Add egg yolks, one at a time, beating well after each addition. Stir in two 1-ounce squares melted unsweetened chocolate. Sift together flour, salt, baking powder, and baking soda. Add to creamed mixture alternately with milk and first 1 teaspoon vanilla. Beat well after each addition. Fold in egg whites till well blended. Spread in 2 waxed-paper-lined 9x1½-inch round pans. Bake at 350° for 18 to 20 minutes. Cool layers thoroughly before filling.

Melt the 8 squares semisweet chocolate over hot water; cool slightly. Whip cream just till *soft* peaks form. Fold in chocolate and toasted almonds. Mixture should be smooth and dark. Spread filling between cake layers.

Melt the one and a half 1-ounce squares unsweetened chocolate and butter or margarine over low heat, stirring constantly. Remove from heat. Stir in confectioners' sugar and remaining 1 teaspoon vanilla till crumbly. Blend in 3 tablespoons boiling water; add more water as needed, a teaspoon at a time, to form medium glaze of pouring consistency (takes about 2 teaspoons). Quickly pour the glaze over top of torte; spread glaze over top and sides.

Surprise Chocolate Torte boasts the favorite combination of coffee and chocolate. The center filling is flavored with instant coffee powder to accent the chocolate cake around it.

Brownie Torte

>   3 egg whites
> ½ teaspoon vanilla
>   Dash salt
> ¾ cup sugar
> ¾ cup fine chocolate-wafer
>   crumbs
> ½ cup chopped walnuts
>   Sweetened whipped cream
>   Chocolate curls

Beat egg whites, vanilla, and salt to soft peaks. Gradually add sugar; beat to stiff peaks. Fold in crumbs and walnuts. Spread in buttered 9-inch pie plate. Bake at 325° for 35 minutes. Cool well; top with whipped cream. Chill 3 to 4 hours. Garnish with chocolate curls.

TORTELLINI—A form of pasta that is related to ravioli in that it is usually served stuffed with a savory filling and topped with a delicious sauce.

Tortellini is made from a dough of durum flour and water, which is shaped into a small, circular form. The nutrients that it provides are carbohydrate, protein, B vitamins, and iron. The filling and sauce increase the nutritional value of tortellini. (See also *Pasta.*)

TORTILLA *(tôr tē′ uh)*—A thin, round, unleavened bread. Tortilla is considered the national bread of Mexico.

Tortillas are made from masa, a cornmeal mixture, or from wheat flour. The dough is rolled into a ball and flattened by patting with the hands or by using a special press. Then, the tortillas are baked on a griddle until done but not browned.

Tortillas are often eaten plain. Plain tortillas are brought to the table piping hot to be eaten as bread with the meal. The tortillas are covered with a napkin or a saucer turned upside down to keep them hot. Often, these tortillas are spread with butter, sprinkled with salt, and rolled into a cylinder before they are eaten.

Frequently, tortillas are used in making other Mexican dishes. They are wrapped around a meat mixture to make enchiladas. When fried crisp, they are called tostadas and are topped with a meat mixture to make a delectable main dish. Crisp tortillas are also the basis for the popular tacos. Both frozen and canned tortillas are available in supermarkets.

Tortillas are sometimes cut into quarters to make tortilla chips. You can prepare them yourself or purchase bags of tortilla chips in the supermarket. They are used with dips or hot sauces for appetizers. The chips are good accompaniments for sandwiches, Mexican-style foods, and soups. You can also use tortilla chips in recipes for sandwiches and appetizers, or use crushed tortilla chips atop casseroles for a flavorful, crunchy topping. (See also *Mexican Cookery*.)

Mexican–Style Cheese Sandwiches

     1 package frozen tortillas (12)
     6 tablespoons butter or margarine,
        softened
     6 ounces Monterey Jack cheese,
        sliced ⅛ inch thick
     1 7¾-ounce can frozen avocado
        dip, thawed

Spread one side of tortillas with butter. For each sandwich, place a tortilla, buttered side down, in skillet or on griddle. Cook till lightly browned. Place cheese slice on top of tortilla. Cover with second tortilla, buttered side up. Turn immediately. Continue cooking till tortilla is lightly browned and cheese melts. Remove from heat; cut sandwich into quarters. Repeat with remaining tortillas. Serve with avocado dip. Makes 6 sandwiches.

TORTONI *(tôr tō′ nē)* — A frozen dessert consisting of whipped cream or ice cream with ingredients such as chopped almonds, cherries, macaroons, and rum, sherry, or a liqueur added for extra flavor.

Tortoni mixtures are often divided into individual servings and frozen in small cups or paper bake cups. This style of dessert is known as biscuit tortoni.

Quick Tortoni Cups

     1 quart vanilla ice cream,
        softened
     ½ cup slivered almonds, toasted
     1 ⅞-ounce milk chocolate candy
        bar
     2 tablespoons chopped maraschino
        cherries
     ½ teaspoon brandy flavoring
     ¼ teaspoon grated orange peel
     ¼ teaspoon grated lemon peel

Blend together all ingredients. Pile the ice cream mixture into 10 paper bake cups in muffin pans. Cover and freeze till firm. Garnish each tortoni with a maraschino cherry flower, if desired. Makes 10 servings.

Garnish Quick Tortoni Cups with cherry flowers. To make flowers, cut whole cherries halfway through and spread petals apart.

Tortoni

       1 tablespoon butter or margarine
    1/3 cup fine vanilla wafer crumbs
       2 tablespoons flaked coconut,
            toasted
    1/4 teaspoon almond extract
       1 pint vanilla ice cream, softened
    1/4 cup apricot preserves
       1 tablespoon chopped, toasted
            almonds

Melt butter; add crumbs, coconut, and almond extract. Put in 6 paper bake cups in muffin pans; top with ice cream and preserves. Sprinkle with almonds. Cover; freeze. Serves 6.

TOSTADA *(tō stä′ duh)* — A crisp tortilla. Tostada also refers to a crisp tortilla topped with a meat mixture, beans, shredded lettuce, chopped vegetables, cheese, and hot sauce, such as in the following recipe for Mexican Beef Tostadas.

Mexican Beef Tostadas

       1 small onion, cut in pieces
       1 clove garlic, halved
       1 pound ground beef
    1/2 teaspoon salt
    1/2 teaspoon chili powder
       8 ounces sharp process American
            cheese, cut in cubes (2 cups)
    1/2 slice bread, torn in pieces
      12 tortillas (canned or frozen)
         Salad oil
         Mexican Fried Beans
       1 small head lettuce, shredded
       2 medium tomatoes, chopped
         Hot Sauce for Tostadas

Put onion and garlic in blender container; blend till coarsely chopped. In skillet cook beef, onion, and garlic till meat is browned. Drain off fat. Add salt and chili powder. Place cheese and bread in blender container; blend till coarsely chopped.

In skillet fry tortillas till crisp in 1/4 inch hot oil. Drain. Spoon about 1/4 cup meat mixture onto each tortilla. Top with Mexican Fried Beans, shredded lettuce, chopped tomato, and cheese. Pass Hot Sauce for Tostadas.

Mexican Fried Beans

Preheat leftovers in hot salad oil to make refried beans—a favorite with Mexican dinners—

       6 slices bacon
       2 15-ounce cans kidney beans
    1/2 teaspoon salt

In a 10-inch skillet cook the bacon slices till they are crisp. Drain the bacon, reserving 2 tablespoons of the bacon drippings.

Put 1 can of the kidney beans *with liquid* in blender container. Put 1/2 teaspoon salt, crisp-cooked bacon, and the 2 tablespoons reserved bacon drippings in blender container. Adjust lid; blend till ingredients are thoroughly combined. (When necessary, stop blender and use rubber spatula to scrape down sides.)

Return bean mixture to skillet. Drain remaining can of kidney beans; stir kidney beans into blended bean mixture in skillet. Mash whole beans slightly. Cook bean mixture, uncovered, over low heat, stirring frequently till mixture is thickened and hot through, about 10 minutes. Serves 4 to 6.

Stack all the meal together for a tostada. Yankee Tostada, a quick version, combines bread, meat, and vegetables in one dish.

Hot Sauce for Tostadas

1 16-ounce can tomatoes
1 tablespoon salad oil
1 small onion, cut in pieces
½ teaspoon dried oregano leaves,
    crushed
1 tablespoon wine vinegar
1 4-ounce can green chilies,
    drained

Drain the tomatoes, reserving 2 tablespoons of the juice. Put tomatoes, reserved juice, oil, onion, oregano, vinegar, and *one* of the green chilies in a blender container. Blend almost smooth. Add more chilies, if desired.

In some variations of the classic tostada combination, corn muffins are used instead of tortillas, as in this recipe. (See also *Mexican Cookery*.)

Yankee Tostada

1 15½-ounce can barbecue sauce and
    beef
½ teaspoon dried oregano leaves,
    crushed
½ teaspoon garlic salt
    Dash cayenne pepper
1 11-ounce jar baked beans in
    molasses sauce
8 toaster-style corn muffins
1½ cups coarsely shredded lettuce
4 ounces sharp Cheddar cheese,
    shredded (1 cup)

Combine the barbecue sauce and beef, oregano, garlic salt, and cayenne pepper; heat through. Meanwhile, heat the baked beans in molasses sauce. Toast corn muffins. Assemble tostadas by topping toasted muffins with hot beans, shredded lettuce, barbecue sauce mixture, and shredded cheese. Makes 8 servings.

TOSS—To mix foods together by lifting and letting them fall lightly. Ingredients are tossed together to combine them or to moisten one with another. For instance, salads are tossed with dressings to coat each piece with the dressing mixture.

TOURNEDOS *(toor' ni dō', tŏŏr' ni dō')*—A beef fillet steak cut from the tenderloin. These lean steaks usually have bacon or a strip of pork fat wrapped around the edge. A piece of string is used to hold the fat in place. The tournedos are then broiled or cooked quickly in butter. The string is removed and the strip of bacon or fat may be removed, too, if desired. When served, the tournedos are placed on a small circle of bread, rice, or potatoes. This foundation absorbs the delicious juices and adds height to the tournedos. A sauce and garnish are added to complete this delicious and elegant entrée.

Tournedos of Beef Della Casa

4 large fresh mushroom caps
¼ cup butter or margarine
¼ cup olive oil *or* salad oil
4 6- to 8-ounce beef fillets,
    about 2 inches thick
    Salt and pepper

• • •

4 thin slices Prosciutto ham
4 slices white bread, toasted
½ cup Béarnaise Sauce
    (See *Béarnaise Sauce*)

In skillet cook mushroom caps in butter and olive oil *or* salad oil for about 3 minutes. Remove mushroom caps from skillet and add fillets. Cook about 10 minutes, turning to brown all sides evenly. Season with salt and pepper. Remove fillets to 10x6x1¾-inch baking dish. Top each fillet with 1 slice Prosciutto ham and a mushroom cap. Bake at 350° for 5 minutes. Cut toasted bread slices to size of fillets. Place each fillet on a slice of toast; top each with 2 tablespoons Béarnaise Sauce. Serves 4.

TRAPPIST CHEESE—A pale yellow, semisoft cheese made originally at the Trappist monastery in Yugoslavia. The flavor of Trappist cheese ranges from mild to strong. The odor is similar to that of a mild Limburger cheese.

Trappist cheese is made from whole milk. Usually it is cow's milk, but occasionally goat or ewe milk is used in addition to the cow's milk. The cheese is cured like a hard cheese and ripened for five to six weeks. The size of Trappist cheeses sent to the markets varies. Some are two to three pounds; others are five, and a few are as large as ten pounds or more.

Trappist cheese is much like Port du Salut cheese of France and Oka cheese of Canada. The similarities are due to the fact that these cheeses also were originated by Trappist monks. (See also *Cheese.*)

TREACLE *(trē′ kuhl)* — Another name for molasses. This name used especially in Great Britain. Mixtures of molasses and corn syrup also are called treacle or golden syrup. (See also *Molasses.*)

TRIFLE *(trī′ fuhl)* — A layered dessert consisting of cake spread with jam or jelly, sprinkled with liquor, covered with custard, and topped with whipped cream. This is an English dessert, but it has been an American favorite since colonial days.

The ingredients in trifle and the order of assembling these ingredients vary. For instance, the cake is usually sponge cake; however, ladyfingers, macaroons, angel cake, pound cake, and stale cake fit into the recipe equally well. The jam or jelly spread on the cake can be any flavor. Apricot, peach, strawberry, and raspberry are among the favorite ones.

This combination of cake and jam is soaked with sherry, brandy, or rum. The liquor adds a delicious flavor and also serves to moisten the cake. This is an especially good feature, as you can make good use of stale cake.

Fruit may be placed atop the liquor-soaked cake in addition to the other ingredients, if desired. Then, a custard is poured over the trifle and it is chilled. When served, whipped cream and a garnish of chopped nuts or candied fruit are sprinkled over the trifle.

Usually, this enticing dessert is served in a pretty glass bowl so as to display the layers. Often, the cake is cut into fingers and arranged spoke-fashion in the bowl for an even more attractive display. (See also *English Cookery.*)

Choose one of your prettiest glass bowls when making Trifle so that the finger sandwiches arranged spoke-fashion will show.

Trifle

1 layer sponge cake *or* ½ tube
  chiffon cake
½ cup raspberry preserves
⅓ to ½ cup dry sherry
1 17-ounce can apricot halves,
  drained
1 3- or 3¼-ounce package *regular*
  vanilla pudding mix
3 cups milk
1 teaspoon vanilla
½ cup whipping cream
¼ cup slivered almonds, toasted

Slice cake into thin fingers. Spread *half* the fingers with preserves and top with remaining fingers to make sandwiches. Place *half* the finger sandwiches, spoke-fashion, in a 2-quart serving dish. Sprinkle with *half* the sherry. Repeat with remaining cake and sherry. Quarter apricots; place atop cake. Cook pudding following package directions, using the 3 cups milk. Stir in vanilla. While pudding is hot, pour over trifle. Chill the dessert thoroughly.

Whip cream. Garnish trifle with whipped cream and toasted almonds. Makes 8 servings.

Tropical Trifle

1 angel loaf cake
¼ cup dry sherry
1 11-ounce can mandarin orange
    sections
¼ cup slivered almonds, toasted
1 3¾-ounce package vanilla
    whipped dessert mix
Toasted, slivered almonds

Cut cake in 1-inch cubes to measure about 9 cups. (Cover and store any extra cake.) Place cake cubes in 11¾x7½x1¾-inch baking dish. Drizzle sherry evenly over cake cubes. Drain mandarin oranges, reserving syrup. Set aside ¼ cup orange sections for garnish; arrange remaining mandarin orange sections over cake. Sprinkle evenly with ¼ cup toasted almonds.

Prepare vanilla whipped dessert mix according to package directions, substituting reserved mandarin orange syrup for the water called for. Pour evenly over cake. Chill thoroughly. To serve, cut in squares; garnish with reserved orange sections and additional toasted almonds, if desired. Makes 6 to 8 servings.

Tropical Trifle uses angel cake cubes as a foundation. Make your own cake, purchase a bakery one, or make use of leftover cake.

TRIPE—The inner lining of the stomach of an animal, which is used for food. Most of the tripe used is from beef; however, some is from oxen, sheep, and goats.

Tripe has been regarded as succulent fare since ancient times. Such historical figures as Homer, the Greek poet, and William the Conqueror are recorded to have praised the tripe dishes served to them. Later in history, the French made tripe into a classic dish by creating tripe à la mode de Caen—a well-seasoned tripe recipe sparked with wines. In modern times, tripe has retained its status as gourmet fare, especially in France, Portugal, and some American cities such as New York and Boston. Many Americans, however, are unfamiliar with tripe.

Today, as in ancient times, there are two types of tripe—plain and honeycomb. The plain tripe is smooth and somewhat rubbery in texture. The honeycomb type has the lacy construction of a honeycomb and is more delicate than is the plain type. Occasionally, another type, pocket tripe, will be identified. This is honeycomb tripe that has not been split open.

Nutritionally, tripe adds protein to the diet. It also contributes minerals and B vitamins, especially riboflavin. A 5x2½-inch piece has 84 calories.

Tripe is available fresh, canned, and pickled. Tripe is partially cooked before being sold. However, it requires precooking before being served. In precooking, tripe is simmered in salted water for about two hours. Then, it is cooked.

You may like to cook the tripe by simply dipping it in a batter and frying, or by basting it with butter or margarine and broiling it. You may, however, prefer a more elaborate preparation such as simmering it in a spicy tomato sauce, baking it with a dressing, creaming the tripe, or making it into the thick soup, pepperpot. (See also *Variety Meat*.)

TROTTER—The foot of an animal, such as a pig, sheep, or cow, used for food.

TRIVET—A stand consisting of a plate with short legs attached. Trivets are used to hold a dish of hot food to protect the table or counter surfaces.

TROUT—A finfish that lives most often in freshwater lakes and streams. It belongs to the family salmonidae, making it a relative of the salmon and whitefish.

Many varieties of this hardy fish are native to the North American continent, although the brown trout was imported to America from Germany in 1883, and a year later, supplemented by a shipment from England. The brown trout, common in Europe, dates back to the fifth century.

Types of trout: There are many varieties of trout, some living in eastern waters and others in western waters. Varieties include rainbow, brown, cutthroat, golden, brook, and lake trout, plus others.

Rainbow trout—Probably the most popular trout, it is rightfully named because of the pink stripe that runs the length of its body. The delicate-colored markings of this flashing trout depend on the environment—food, water temperature, season, and composition of the water. This is true for many other trout varieties.

The rainbow is a sport fish that used to be taken only along the Pacific coast from Mexico to Alaska. Now, it is found across the United States and Canada.

When the rainbow finds its way to the ocean, it is called a steelhead. It migrates great distances from streams to the ocean and then returns to its native stream to spawn, like salmon. Unlike salmon, however, not all of the steelheads die after they finish spawning.

The average rainbow trout weighs between two and eight pounds; some get as large as 30 to 40 pounds, particularly those that live in the ocean.

Brown trout—Sometimes called Loch Leven or brownie, this adaptable, hardy fish averages around seven or eight pounds and is able to withstand slightly warmer water than most trout. When the brown trout was first introduced to North Ameri-can waters, many fishermen disliked this particular variety, thinking it would kill off other types of trout. However, the brown trout has proven adaptable.

Cutthroat trout—Known by more than 70 names, the cutthroat is found in the Rocky Mountains and west to the Pacific from southern Alaska to California. This fish also migrates to the sea but stays close to the mouth of the river. It has a red or orange slash on the lower jaw, and the average length of this fish is from 10 to 15 inches for inland fish and about 16 inches for the ocean variety.

Golden trout—Normally found in high altitude lakes of California, Idaho, Oregon, Montana, Wyoming, and Washington, high above the timberline in rugged mountains, golden trout is one of the prettiest of trout. It weighs about one pound.

Brook trout—Often referred to as the speckled trout, this is a favorite game fish that lives in clear, cold streams and lakes. The flesh can vary from white to deep red, depending on the fish's diet. Heredity also plays a part in the color of the flesh for this fish. Brook trout average between one and two pounds. Some of the fish living in the rivers along the coast migrate to the sea. When brook trout migrate to the sea, they are called sea trout.

Lake trout—The granddaddy of them all, lake trout is the largest fish of the group and is native to North America.

Other types of trout include the splake, a cross between the lake and brook trout, the arctic charr, and the Dolly Varden.

Nutritional value: Trout is a source of protein, with one 3½-ounce serving (uncooked) giving a good share of the day's protein requirement. The same sized portion of uncooked brook trout equals 101 calories, of rainbow trout equals 195 calories, and of lake trout adds 241 calories.

How to select: Fishermen can catch trout in many lakes, rivers, and streams, or trout can be purchased fresh or frozen, either drawn, dressed, or cut into fillets. Smoked trout is also available. Fresh trout that are purchased dressed (scaled and eviscerated) usually weigh between one-third and two pounds.

Trout at their best

← What fisherman wouldn't be proud to serve cornmeal-coated Brookside-Fried Trout sizzling hot from the skillet.

The dressed fish that is purchased fresh should have elastic, firm flesh, mild odor, bright, clear eyes, and shiny skin. Frozen trout should be solidly frozen without evidence of frost on the inside or outside of the package or signs of freezer burn.

How to store: Keep cleaned fresh trout chilled until cooked. Freshly caught fish can be placed on a snowbank in the high mountains or in thermal-type wicker fish baskets or insulated ice chests. As soon as possible, store fresh trout in the refrigerator and use within a day or two for fish of best quality.

Keep trout frozen solid in the freezer until ready to use. Do not freeze fish longer than six months, for prolonged storage affects flavor, texture, and color.

How to use: Since some trout are considered fat fish and others lean fish, most any preparation method can be used when cooking this fish. Europeans often cook trout in water to which vinegar has been added. This makes the skin bluer and the flesh of the fish whiter.

Many times, trout is prepared over a campfire near the stream where it is caught. By cooking trout at the peak of freshness, the flavor will be at its very best. Back home, trout can be coated and fried in a skillet, stuffed and baked, broiled, or poached. (See also *Fish.*)

Brookside Fried Trout

6 fresh or frozen pan-dressed
trout (about ½ pound each)
⅔ cup yellow cornmeal
¼ cup all-purpose flour
2 teaspoons salt
½ teaspoon paprika
Shortening

Thaw fish if frozen; dry with paper toweling. Combine cornmeal, flour, salt, and paprika. Coat fish with mixture. In skillet heat a little shortening over *hot* coals until shortening is melted and hot. Cook fish till lightly browned, about 4 minutes on each side. Fish is done when the cooked meat flakes easily when tested with a fork. Makes 6 servings.

Sesame Rainbow Trout

Prepare the sauce ahead of time and take it in a jar to a picnic—

4 fresh or frozen pan-dressed
rainbow trout (about ½ pound
each)
Salt and pepper
¼ cup salad oil
2 tablespoons toasted sesame seed
2 tablespoons lemon juice
½ teaspoon salt
Dash pepper

Thaw fish if frozen; dry with paper toweling. Season generously with salt and pepper. Wrap tails with greased foil. Place in well-greased wire broiler basket. Combine salad oil, sesame seed, lemon juice, ½ teaspoon salt, and dash pepper. Brush fish, inside and out, with the sesame mixture. Grill about 4 inches from *medium-hot* coals for 8 to 10 minutes. Repeat brushing. Turn and grill till fish flakes easily when tested with a fork, about 8 to 10 minutes longer. Remove foil. Makes 4 servings.

Trout with Salami Topping

An unusual combination of flavors—

4 fresh or frozen pan-dressed
trout (about ½ pound each)
⅓ cup all-purpose flour
½ teaspoon paprika
¼ teaspoon salt
Dash pepper
½ cup butter or margarine
4 ounces sliced salami
1 tablespoon lemon juice

Thaw fish if frozen; dry with paper toweling. Combine flour, paprika, salt, and pepper. Roll fish in flour mixture. In a large, heavy skillet melt the butter. Place fish in skillet in a single layer. Fry till browned on one side, 4 to 5 minutes. Turn carefully. Brown second side and cook till fish flakes easily when tested with a fork, about 4 to 5 minutes longer. Remove fish to platter; keep warm. Cut salami into thin strips. Cook salami in butter in skillet for 1 to 2 minutes. Stir in lemon juice. Spoon over cooked fish. Makes 4 servings.

TRUFFLE *(truf' uhl, trōō' fuhl)* — **1.** The edible part of certain fungus that grows underground. **2.** A chocolate candy that is formed into balls.

The fungus type of truffle is round with a rough, wrinkled appearance. Its size varies from that of a walnut to an orange, and the colors of the skin range from white to black. Truffles grow in the soil around the roots of oak trees in some European countries. Considered the finest type are the dark brown or black truffles of the Perigord region of France. At the opposite end of the spectrum, the white truffles from Italy's Piedmont area are also highly regarded.

Because they cannot be cultivated, truffles must be found wild. Therefore, they are relatively scarce, making them exceedingly expensive. Well-trained pigs and dogs are used to sniff out and retrieve the fungus from where it grows.

Truffles have little nutritive value and are added to such mixtures as *pâté de foie gras* or *truite farcie* for their delicate flavor. Truffles are also thinly sliced when used for decorations.

In the United States, canned truffles are available cooked and ready to serve.

The candy type of truffle is a solid chocolate candy shaped into small balls. They are commonly coated with grated chocolate or small chocolate decorative candies. (See also *French Cookery.*)

Truite Farcie

   6 fresh mushrooms, thinly sliced
   2 leeks, cut in julienne strips
   1 medium carrot, cut in julienne strips
   1 medium celery branch, cut in julienne strips
   1 truffle, thinly sliced
   ¼ cup butter or margarine
   ¼ cup port
   2 tablespoons cognac *or* brandy
   2 tablespoons dry vermouth
   6 pan-dressed trout, boned
   1 cup dry white wine
      Court Bouillon
   4 egg yolks
   ½ cup whipping cream

Cook mushrooms, leeks, carrot, celery, and truffle in ¼ cup butter for 2 to 3 minutes. Add port, cognac, and dry vermouth. Cook about 2 minutes longer or till liquid is reduced to a glaze. Season inside of trout with salt and pepper. Stuff with vegetable mixture. In skillet simmer fish in enough white wine to cover (about 1 cup) till fish flakes easily with a fork, about 5 minutes. Remove fish to hot platter and keep warm while preparing sauce.

To make sauce, in top of double boiler combine 1 cup Court Bouillon with egg yolks and whipping cream. Beat over *hot, not boiling* water till thickened. Season with salt and pepper. Pour over stuffed trout. Sprinkle with paprika and garnish with lemon wedges, if desired. Makes 6 servings.

Court Bouillon: In a saucepan combine ¼ cup chopped celery, ¼ cup chopped carrot, and ¼ cup chopped onion. Add 2 cups water, 1 tablespoon white vinegar, 1½ teaspoons snipped parsley, 1 teaspoon salt, 2 peppercorns, 1 small bay leaf, and 1 whole clove. Bring to boiling; reduce heat and simmer, uncovered, till liquid is reduced to one-half (1 cup). Strain before using. (Try poaching fish in the Court Bouillon for a wonderful herb flavor.)

TRUSS — To fasten openings, wings, and legs of poultry or game birds with skewers and string. This keeps the bird in a compact shape during roasting.

TRYING OUT — Another term for rendering animal fat by slow heating to separate the fat from connective tissue. The crisp bits of tissue that remain after the fat is poured off are called cracklings.

TUBE PAN — A round baking pan used for angel food cakes, sponge-type cakes, and some desserts. It has a tube in the center, which aids in heat penetration of the cake during baking. Many types of tube pans also have removable bottoms that make it easier to remove the baked cake from the pan. Some pans even have feet on the top rim so that the pan can be inverted for the cooling of delicately structured cakes. Otherwise, the tube part can be slipped over the neck of a bottle as the pan is inverted. Fluted tube pans and Turk's head pans are variations of the tube pan.

Make the main dish Tuna-Bean Salad. The dressing is a blend of olive oil and wine vinegar subtly seasoned with mustard.

TUNA — A large food fish that lives in packs or schools in the warmer saltwater areas of the Atlantic and Pacific oceans and the Mediterranean Sea. The tuna, also called horse mackerel or tunny, is a member of the mackerel family.

In the Mediterranean area many hundreds of years before Christ, tuna was considered a delicacy and was eaten by the rich nobles. This particular fish was also found in the decorations and designs of early Greek pottery. The ancient Greek word for tuna was "thunnos," very close to the modern-day name, tuna.

In the Americas, the Incas were catching tuna long before Columbus landed. Off the coast of Peru, fishing for tuna in the Pacific was advanced, even as early as 1531, when the conquistadors arrived.

In the early 1900s, the fledgling tuna industry received a boost by the disappearance of sardine from the California coast. Ten years later, this industry was further stimulated by the need for food during the First World War. The scarcity of other foods and the fact that tuna was both nutritious and inexpensive, made tuna a favorite with the public.

At first, the albacore was most popular, but later the other light meat tunas joined in the popularity. By 1953, tuna had become the most favored canned fish, just 50 years after it was first canned.

Processing of tuna: Since the tuna is such a large fish, some is sold in steaks, either fresh or frozen, but the majority of the catch is sold canned.

The canning process starts on the boats after the tuna are caught. Spotting schools of tuna is not an easy task. Some people use airplanes to spot the fish. Large nets called "purse seines" are used to catch large numbers of fish at one time. After they are caught, the tuna are then frozen immediately on board the boat. This has to be done because these boats may stay out as long as 30 to 45 days before delivering their catch to canners.

At the cannery, the tuna is thawed, prepared for cooking, sorted according to size, cooked, and cooled. The skin, bones, and dark meat are removed. What is left of the fish is separated into quarters, ready to be packed into cans. Salt and vegetable oil are added. Then, the can is sealed, processed, cooled, labeled, and shipped to local supermarkets.

Types of tuna: There are four major varieties of tuna. The first is albacore, the only tuna that can be labeled white meat. The fish ranges between 10 and 60 pounds and lives in the Pacific waters from Mexico to southern California.

Another variety of tuna is the yellowfin, which has light meat. It is a larger fish than the albacore with the best weight for canning being between 40 and 100 pounds. It, too, lives in the Pacific as far south as northern Chile.

The skipjack is the smallest tuna and it has light meat. This fish can be distinguished from other tuna because of its parallel stripes on the lower sides. Skipjack tuna weigh between 4 and 24 pounds.

A bluefin tuna is found in both Atlantic and Pacific waters and is considered a real sport fish in the Atlantic because it can weigh up to 1,000 pounds and can put up quite a fight when caught. Pacific bluefin average around 80 pounds.

Nutritional value: Tuna is a good source of protein. It also contains phosphorus, iron, and some of the B vitamins. The tuna packed in oil also has some vitamin A. Drained tuna, which has been packed in oil, has about 160 calories per half-cup serving, whereas water-pack tuna, drained, has about 127 calories for a half-cup serving. For fresh tuna, a 3½-ounce serving (uncooked) of bluefin tuna adds about 145 calories to the diet, while yellowfin tuna adds 133 calories to the diet.

Fat from the tuna is high in polyunsaturated fatty acids, making it good for low cholesterol diets. When packed in oil, the oil used is of the vegetable variety. In addition, tuna is easily digested because it is low in connective tissue.

How to select: Tuna can be purchased in steaks, fresh or frozen, and canned. The fresh steaks should have a fresh-cut appearance—not dried out around the edges It should have little fish odor. The frozen tuna should be tightly wrapped and solidly frozen when purchased and should have little, if any, fish odor.

Canned tuna comes in several packs. Some tuna, called dietetic pack, is canned in distilled water with no salt. Other tuna is packed in vegetable oil or water. Some tuna, called *tonno,* is packed in olive oil, and has more salt included.

Tuna also comes canned in various-sized pieces. The most expensive style of tuna is fancy or solid-pack tuna. The can will contain three or four large pieces and should be used when appearance is important. The medium-priced tuna is called chunk-style and is made up of small pieces. Use chunk tuna for casseroles where nice-sized pieces are important. The least expensive tuna is grated or flaked. The pieces are small and irregular and are best for use in sandwich spreads and dips where appearance is not as important as for some dishes.

Look on the label of the can to see whether the meat is white (albacore) or light, in addition to the size of the pieces—solid, chunk, grated, or flaked.

How to store: Store fresh tuna in the refrigerator and use it within a short period of time for best flavor. Usually, a day or two after purchase is the maximum time for keeping fresh tuna.

Store frozen fish in the freezer, wrapped and sealed. Do not freeze tuna longer than six months for best quality.

Canned tuna should be stored on the shelf in a cool, dry place.

How to use: Because tuna is considered a fat fish, fresh tuna can be prepared by any of the cooking methods that are used for other fat fish, including baking, broiling, frying, and poaching.

Canned tuna is an inexpensive source of protein, and it can be used to produce a budget-stretching meal that is mouth-watering. Canned tuna is versatile and the flavor is popular among all age groups. It can be used in a variety of ways—in hearty soups and chowders, sandwich fillings, hot main dishes, casseroles, appetizers, and salads. (See also *Fish.*)

Use chunk-style tuna in Tuna-Broccoli Casserole for nice-sized pieces of fish. Individual ramekins make serving a snap.

Tuna-Bean Salad

    1 cup dry navy beans
    3 cups cold water
    1 teaspoon salt
    ¼ cup olive oil
    ¼ cup white wine vinegar
    ½ teaspoon dry mustard
    ½ teaspoon salt
      Dash pepper
    1 6½-, 7-, or 9¼-ounce can tuna,
      chilled and drained
    1 small red onion, thinly sliced
      Lettuce
    1 tablespoon snipped parsley

Rinse dry navy beans. Add to 3 cups cold water and soak overnight. Add 1 teaspoon salt to beans and soaking water. Cover and bring to a boil. Reduce heat and simmer until beans are tender, about 1 hour. Drain and chill.

In screw-top jar combine olive oil, wine vinegar, dry mustard, ½ teaspoon salt, and pepper. Cover and shake well. Chill. Shake thoroughly again just before using.

Combine beans, tuna, and the sliced onion, separated into rings. Drizzle with dressing. Toss lightly. Serve in a lettuce-lined bowl. Sprinkle with parsley. Makes 4 servings.

Packaged stuffing cubes add toasty crispness and delicate herb flavor to creamy Tuna and Croutons—perfect for supper.

Tuna Salad Bake

Combine one 10½-ounce can condensed cream of chicken soup, 1 cup diced celery, ¼ cup finely chopped onion, ½ cup mayonnaise or salad dressing, ½ teaspoon salt, and dash pepper. Fold in one 6½- or 7-ounce can tuna, drained and flaked, and 3 hard-cooked eggs, sliced. Turn into a 1½-quart casserole. Sprinkle with 1 cup crushed potato chips. Bake at 400° for 35 minutes. Makes 4 servings.

Tuna-Broccoli Casseroles

    2 10-ounce packages frozen chopped
      broccoli
    6 tablespoons butter or margarine
    ½ cup all-purpose flour
    3½ cups milk
    ⅓ cup grated Parmesan cheese
    2 tablespoons lemon juice
    ¼ teaspoon dried dillweed
    1 9¼-ounce can tuna, drained
      and broken up

Cook broccoli according to package directions; drain. In saucepan melt butter over low heat. Blend in flour and 1 teaspoon salt. Add milk all at once. Cook and stir till thickened and bubbly. Add Parmesan, lemon juice, and dillweed. Stir in broccoli and tuna.

Turn tuna mixture into 8 individual casseroles. Bake at 375° for 25 minutes. Sprinkle with snipped parsley, if desired. Serves 8.

Tuna and Croutons

Cook one 10-ounce package frozen chopped spinach according to package directions; drain well. Spread in 10x6x1¾-inch baking dish.

Melt 2 tablespoons butter in saucepan. Blend in 3 tablespoons all-purpose flour, ½ teaspoon salt, and dash cayenne. Gradually stir in 1½ cups milk and ½ cup light cream. Cook and stir till thick and bubbly. Add 2 ounces process Swiss cheese, shredded (½ cup); stir till melted. Stir in two 6½- or 7-ounce cans tuna, drained and broken up. Pour over spinach layer. Toss 1½ cups packaged seasoned stuffing croutons with 1½ tablespoons melted butter. Sprinkle around border of casserole. Bake at 375° for 25 to 30 minutes. Makes 6 servings.

Company Creamed Tuna

    2 tablespoons finely chopped
        onion
    3 tablespoons butter
    3 tablespoons all-purpose flour
    ¼ teaspoon salt
      Dash pepper
 1¼ cups milk
    ½ cup dairy sour cream
    1 6½- or 7-ounce can tuna,
        drained
    3 tablespoons dry white wine
    2 tablespoons snipped parsley
      Toasted slivered almonds
      Pastry shells *or* buttered
        toast points

In blazer pan of chafing dish cook onion in butter till tender but not brown. Blend in flour, salt, and pepper. Add milk all at once; cook quickly, stirring constantly, until mixture thickens and bubbles. Stir in sour cream. Add tuna, wine, and ·parsley. Heat through. Set blazer pan on top of bain-marie over flame.· Sprinkle toasted almonds over sauce. Spoon into pastry shells or over hot buttered toast points. Makes 4 servings.

Tuna Supper Dish

    1 cup soft bread crumbs
    4 tablespoons butter or margarine
    1 9-ounce package frozen Italian
        green beans
    2 tablespoons all-purpose flour
 1⅓ cups chicken broth
    ⅛ teaspoon ground nutmeg
      Dash pepper
    2 6½- or 7-ounce cans chunk-style
        tuna, drained
    1 cup shredded process American
        cheese (4 ounces)

In heavy skillet toast the bread crumbs in *2 tablespoons* of the butter till golden brown. Set aside. Cook beans according to package directions; drain. In skillet melt remaining 2 tablespoons butter; blend in flour. Add chicken broth, nutmeg, and pepper. Cook and stir till thick and smooth. Add tuna, cheese, and beans; reduce heat. Simmer till cheese melts. Sprinkle with toasted crumbs. Serves 4 to 6.

Tuna Omelet

    3 tablespoons salad oil
    ½ cup frozen peas
    ½ cup bean sprouts, drained
    1 6½- or 7-ounce can tuna, drained
    6 eggs
    ¼ cup water

In heavy 10-inch skillet heat the oil. (Electric skillet 350°.) Add peas, sprouts, and tuna; cook, stirring ocasionally, till peas are tender, about 5 minutes. Beat eggs with water, ½ teaspoon salt, and dash pepper; pour into skillet. Reduce heat (220°); cook till eggs are set. When almost cooked but still shiny, loosen edges; fold one half over. Serves 4 to 6.

Tuna Patties with Cranberry Sauce

    2 eggs
    ¼ cup milk
 1½ cups soft bread crumbs
    1 tablespoon chopped green onion
    ¼ teaspoon salt
      Dash pepper
    1 9½-ounce can tuna, drained and
        flaked
    1 tablespoon water
    ½ cup fine dry bread crumbs
    2 tablespoons salad oil
    1 8-ounce can whole cranberry sauce

Combine *one* of the eggs, milk, soft bread crumbs, green onion, salt, and pepper. Mix well. Stir in tuna. Form into 6 patties, ¾ inch thick. Beat together remaining egg and water. Dip patties in egg, then in dry bread crumbs. In skillet brown the patties over medium heat in hot oil, about 5 minutes. (Electric skillet 350°.) At serving time, spoon cranberry sauce over each patty. Makes 6 servings.

Tuna-Fruit Salad

Combine one 16-ounce can grapefruit and orange sections, chilled and drained; one 13½-ounce can pineapple tidbits, chilled and drained; one 6½- or 7-ounce can tuna, chilled, drained, and flaked; and ⅓ cup coarsely chopped walnuts. Add ⅓ cup mayonnaise or salad dressing. Toss lightly. Makes 4 servings.

Tuna-Lemon Loaf

Place 4 thin lemon slices in a row in the bottom of a well-greased 8½x4½x2½-inch loaf dish. Combine two 6½- or 7-ounce cans tuna, drained and flaked, with one 10½-ounce can condensed cream of celery soup, 3 beaten egg yolks, 1 cup fine cracker crumbs, ¼ cup finely chopped onion, 2 tablespoons chopped, canned pimiento, 2 tablespoons snipped parsley, 1 tablespoon lemon juice, and dash pepper.

Fold in 3 stiff-beaten egg whites. Spoon mixture over lemon slices in dish. Bake at 350° till center is firm, 45 minutes. Invert on platter. Trim with parsley. Serves 6.

Company Tuna Bake

    1 3-ounce package cream cheese,
        softened
    1 10½-ounce can condensed cream
        of mushroom soup
    1 6½-, 7-, or 9¼-ounce can tuna,
        drained and flaked
    1 tablespoon chopped, canned
        pimiento
    1 tablespoon chopped onion
    1 teaspoon prepared mustard
    ⅓ cup milk
    ½ 7-ounce package (1 cup) elbow
        macaroni, cooked and drained
    ½ cup fine dry bread crumbs
    2 tablespoons butter, melted

Blend cheese into soup, using electric or rotary beater. Stir in next 6 ingredients. Pour into a 1½-quart casserole. Mix crumbs and butter; sprinkle over top. Bake at 375° till hot, about 35 to 40 minutes. Trim with parsley, if desired. Makes 4 or 5 servings.

Broiled Tuna Burgers

Combine one 6½- or 7-ounce can tuna, drained and flaked; 2 tablespoons chopped onion; 2 tablespoons chopped sweet pickle; and ¼ cup mayonnaise or salad dressing.

Split and toast 5 hamburger buns. Butter bottom halves; spread with tuna mixture. Top each with slice of sharp process American cheese. Broil 5 inches from heat till cheese melts, 4 minutes. Add bun tops. Makes 5.

Identify turban squash by its flattened shape and turbanlike top. It's delightful when cut in serving pieces and baked.

TURBAN SQUASH—A flattened, reddish orange, turban-shaped, hard-shelled, winter squash. It is 8 to 10 inches long and 12 to 15 inches across, and the blossom end is striped. As with other winter squash, choose one that is heavy for its size. Store in a cool place. (See also *Squash*.)

Spiced Turban Squash

    2 small turban squash
    ¼ cup honey
    2 tablespoons butter, melted
    1 teaspoon salt
    ½ teaspoon ground ginger
    ¼ teaspoon ground nutmeg
        Dash pepper

Cut the turban squash in quarters; remove the seeds. Place the squash, cut side down, in shallow baking dish. Bake at 375° for 30 minutes. Turn the squash cut side up. Combine the remaining ingredients; spoon over squash. Bake till squash is tender, about 25 to 30 minutes longer. Makes 8 servings.

TURBOT *(tûr' buht)*—A flatfish from European waters that is a member of the flounder family. It is a large fish, weighing about 10 pounds. The white, firm, flaky meat is excellent when poached and served with a sauce. (See also *Flounder*.)